The Work of Intermediate Appellate Courts

The Work of
Intermediate Appellate Courts

The volume of appeals is a commonly used indicator of the demands placed on IACs. Growth in the number of appeals creates the need for greater productivity and provides the justification for the expansion of court resources. Volume is also a measure for comparing the amount of work performed by different IACs. Yet despite the reliance placed on this indicator, volume captures only part of the complexities surrounding the business of IACs, which must be understood if case processing is to be analyzed in a meaningful manner. Clarifying the type and amount of the demands on IACs poses three questions that the concept of volume does not address fully.

- What kinds of cases and issues can be raised on appeal?
- Are some cases and issues raised more frequently than others?
- What portion of the cases settle and what portion require a decision on the merits?

These questions focus attention on three interrelated topics: subject matter jurisdiction, caseload composition, and case attrition.

A court's subject matter jurisdiction influences the number of appeals that are filed. For example, the extent to which guilty pleas and sentencing issues are subject to appeal affects the criminal caseload. The composition of the appellate caseload is important to know because some appeals may move through the process more quickly than others. It may be expected, for example, that appeals arising from jury trials require more time to process than appeals arising from motions. Finally, it is important to know if a funnel analogy in the attrition of appeals after filing can be applied to the caseflow of appeals, as this analogy is used to characterize the flow of cases at the trial level (see President's Commission, 1967). Does the appellate process begin with a large number of appeals at the filing stage (mouth of the funnel), but, just as a funnel becomes narrower, do only a fraction of the appeals filed come out at the decision stage (end of the funnel) because appeals are settled, withdrawn, or abandoned? Because appeals that wash out make fewer demands on the court, it is important to distinguish the appeals that are filed from the number of appeals that a court must decide.

This chapter describes and compares the work confronting each of the four courts. What are the similarities and differences in jurisdiction, caseload composition, and attrition? What are the implications of the observed patterns for the consideration of special procedures and for the processing of cases?

Jurisdiction

All four courts have primarily mandatory subject-matter jurisdiction, hearing appeals of right filed from judgments of the general jurisdiction trial court. None hear appeals in death penalty cases. Although the subject matter jurisdiction of the four courts is basically the same, there are important differences in two main areas: nontrial criminal matters and agency review.

In all courts except Maryland, criminal defendants may challenge by appeal the length or computation of a sentence. In Maryland, such issues may only be raised before a review panel of trial court judges. This means that the Maryland court lacks a category of appeals that constitutes a sizable part of the caseload of the other courts. Appeals raising only sentencing issues (i.e., challenges to the proceeding as well as to the length or computation of the sentence) constituted 30 percent of the criminal appeals in New Jersey, almost 25 percent of the criminal appeals in Florida, but less than 6 percent in Maryland. In Arizona, where *Anders* briefs[7] are filed in 55 percent of the criminal appeals, 20 percent of the remaining criminal appeals raise only sentencing issues.

In all the courts except Maryland, appeals from guilty pleas and from trial court denials of postconviction relief fall within the court's mandatory jurisdiction and constitute a sizable part of the criminal appeals caseload (see Table 2). In Maryland, such appeals are discretionary as a result of a statutory change enacted in 1983 to relieve the court of the growing burden these appeals posed.

Finally, although all four courts hear appeals from decisions of administrative agencies, the appeal path and the type of agency appeals that may be heard differ. In Florida and New Jersey, appeals from administrative agencies go directly to the IAC. In Arizona, the appeal path varies, with high-volume industrial commission and unemployment board appeals going directly to the IAC in Phoenix. In Maryland, appeals go from the agency to the trial court, then to the IAC. This latter appeal path can be expected to reduce the volume of such appeals in the IAC as well as provide it with a previously digested record.

A court's subject matter jurisdiction results from external policy decisions, as reflected in state constitutions and statutes. Jurisdictional arrangements can and do evolve over time, however, with direct and often dramatic effects on the volume of appeals coming to the IAC. Such a change occurred in Maryland in 1983, when mandatory appeals from guilty plea convictions and from denials of postconviction relief were eliminated, reducing the volume of criminal appeals sharply. More recently, Arizona has seen its caseload increase as a result of the transfer of what had been part of the mandatory jurisdiction of the state COLR—review of capital prosecutions in which the death penalty was not imposed and interlocutory appeals.

The implications of these findings regarding subject matter jurisdiction are twofold: First, significant differences in subject matter jurisdiction need to be taken into account when making cross-court comparisons. By inquiring into the subject matter jurisdiction of different courts, clues may be obtained on likely differences in caseload composition. Second, the specific differences among the courts in jurisdiction over sentencing highlight the emergence of these issues as a relevant topic to many courts. Although all IACs may not review issues relating to the computation and length of sentences, this topic merits systematic empirical investigation because of its significance in courts such as Arizona, Florida, and New Jersey.[8]

For the past several years, many states have experienced fundamental changes in sentencing laws with the adoption of sentencing commissions, guidelines, and alternative forms of determinate sentencing. Consequently, appellate courts review sentences without the benefit of any systematic empirical research on the frequency, type, and outcomes of sentencing issues. Because sentencing issues arise in an appreciable proportion of cases, even in states with indeterminate sentencing laws, review of these issues by appeals courts warrants investigation in future research.

Caseload Composition

Caseload composition reflects both an appellate court's subject matter jurisdiction and the nature and volume of its trial courts' activity. Appeal rates are presumed to be lower in civil cases than in criminal cases, where defendants, most of whom are indigent, have appointed counsel and do not bear the economic costs of the appeal. However, there is no systematic and little anecdotal information on appeal rates in particular categories of litigation, a subject also beyond the scope of this research.

Relative Frequency of Criminal and Civil Appeals

One dimension on which caseload composition can be examined is the relative frequency of civil and criminal appeals. The experiences of individual courts suggest that neither category of appeal is universally the faster growing. The four courts under study fall into two patterns. In the first, the caseload is predominantly civil at filing; in the second, it is predominantly criminal. However, because of a higher attrition rate for civil appeals, both before and after submission of the trial court record, all four courts decide more criminal appeals than civil appeals.

In Maryland and New Jersey, the ratio of the number of civil appeals filed to criminal appeals filed is 58 to 42. Although civil appeals in both courts have higher attrition before submission of the trial court record (i.e., docketing) than do criminal appeals, the docketed civil appeals outnumber docketed criminal appeals by a ratio of 53 to 47. The attrition of civil appeals continues, however, and by the decision stage, criminal appeals decided on the merits outnumber civil merits decisions 53 to 47. In Arizona and Florida, on the other hand, criminal appeals outnumber civil appeals at both filing and docketing. Because of the higher attrition rate among civil appeals, criminal appeals become even more preponderant at the decision stage. Specifically, the ratio of decided criminal appeals to decided civil appeals in Florida is 62 to 38; in Arizona, where large numbers of briefed civil appeals were transferred to the Arizona Court of Appeals, Division Two, in Tucson, the ratio is 69 to 31.

Underlying Trial Court Proceeding and Area of Law

In part reflecting differences in subject matter jurisdiction, there are differences in the distribution of the underlying trial court proceeding of decided appeals. This variation is observed across courts and within a court when comparing civil and criminal appeals. As seen in **Table 1**, appeals from jury trials constitute a small percentage of decided civil appeals in all courts (6 to 11 percent). Appeals from nonjury trials (including those in domestic cases) range from a low of 23 percent in Arizona to approximately 40 percent in the other three courts. Appeals from dispositions on pretrial motions constitute 20 to 28 percent of the caseload in all courts except in Florida, where 44 percent of

Table 1
Underlying Trial Court Proceeding
in Decided Civil Appeals

	Arizona	Florida	Maryland	New Jersey
Jury Trials	6%	9%	11%	11%
Nonjury Trials	23	40	42	38
Pretrial Motions	20	44	28	23
Agency Review	46	6	12	26
Other	4	1	6	1
	n=207	n=341	n=265	n=351

the appellate caseload arises from lower court decisions on motions. The greatest variation across courts, however, is in the frequency of appeals from administrative agencies. This ranges from a low of 6 percent in Florida to a high of 46 percent in Arizona (an unusually high figure due to the transfer of private-party civil appeals to the Arizona Court of Appeals, Division Two, in Tucson). Such appeals constitute 12 percent of decided civil appeals in Maryland and 26 percent in New Jersey.

On the criminal side, information presented in **Table 2** indicates that appeals from jury trials constitute a large percentage of the appeals in three courts. A majority of Maryland's appeals come from jury trials; a plurality do so in New Jersey and Florida; but only 18 percent of Arizona's criminal appeals follow jury trials. This variance corresponds to differences between Arizona and the rest of the courts in the percentage of appeals arising from guilty pleas. In Arizona, appeals from guilty pleas account for 51 percent of the caseload. The respective percentages in all the other courts are far smaller—23 percent in Florida, 26 percent in New Jersey, and 1 percent in Maryland, where such appeals are discretionary.

There are two implications to this information. First, an understanding of the caseload composition reveals that there may be conflicting pressures within a court that affect case processing time. For example, Maryland avoids categories of appeals that constitute a sizable part of the criminal appeals caseload in other courts. Maryland does not receive sentencing appeals, and there is no direct appeal from guilty pleas, which when combined with sentence review burden other courts. On the other hand, Maryland has a higher percentage of criminal appeals coming from trials than the other courts. To the extent that more issues are raised in appeals from trials than in appeals from other proceedings, Maryland's burden is greater than the other courts. Thus, knowledge of caseload composition exposes the complexities of the relation-

Table 2
Underlying Trial Court Proceeding
in Decided Criminal Appeals

	Arizona	Florida	Maryland	New Jersey
Jury Trials	18%	41%	64%	44%
Nonjury Trials	3	10	21	20
Guilty Pleas	51	26	1	23
Probation Revocation Hearings	10	12	13`	5
Other	17	11	2	8
	n=383	n=345	n=310	n=283

ship between caseload and case processing. An understanding of why some courts are more expeditious than others is a product of subtle factors that volume alone does not reveal.

The second implication is that there is a critical need for systematic information on the appeal rates across the country. The conventional wisdom is that appeal rates can be estimated by using the number of trials in a given jurisdiction as the denominator and the number of appeals filed as the numerator. However, this approach assumes that the common underlying court proceeding for appeals is a trial.

The information in Table 2 illustrates the limitations of that assumption. Guilty pleas are driving the majority of appeals in Arizona and an appreciable number in Florida and New Jersey. Moreover, other evidence suggests that Arizona is not necessarily an extreme case. Prior research indicates that 40 percent of the appeals in California arise from guilty pleas (Hanson and Chapper, 1988) and that 43 percent of New York City's appeals come from guilty pleas (Wasserman, 1988 at ch. 4, p. 13). If guilty pleas are accounting for large numbers of appeals in several states, especially the populous ones, this would explain why some researchers (e.g., Marvell and Lindgren, 1985) have found no correlation between trial rates and the growth in appeals. Because the rate of appeal is the missing link between the trial and appellate court systems, future research needs to explore this issue.

In contrast to the sharp intercourt differences in the underlying trial court proceeding, the four-court pattern reveals smaller differences in the underlying area of law of the appeals that they must decide. Table 3 indicates that in civil cases the distribution of casetypes by area of law is similar in Florida, Maryland, and New Jersey, where contract/commercial cases constitute the largest percentage of appeals. The next largest categories of cases are domestic relations and torts, which are of nearly equal volume. Arizona's pattern is somewhat different

Table 3
Area of Law for Decided Civil Appeals

	Arizona	Florida	Maryland	New Jersey
Contract/Commercial	16%	32%	24%	26%
Domestic Relations	10	25	23	18
Tort	11	22	18	22
Administrative	40	6	18	24
Property	8	5	8	2
Other	13	11	9	9
	n=153	n=330	n=367	n=375

because during the time under study it transfered some fully briefed private-party appeals to Tucson. Its caseload, after the transfers to Tucson, has a higher percentage of agency cases than the other three courts.

As shown in **Table 4**, the criminal appeals pattern parallels the intercourt similarity in civil appeals. The most frequent serious offense category at conviction is crimes against the person other than homicide. This holds true in each court. Drug offenses account for one-quarter of the offenses in two courts and one-sixth in the other two. However, drug cases on appeal appear to be on the rise because of their increased prosecution at the trial level. Data gathered from five first-level appeals courts during an earlier time period (1983-85) indicated that in one court drug offenses accounted for 10 percent of appeals and smaller percentages in the others (Chapper and Hanson, 1989). Consequently, the information in this report, which is based on appeals filed in 1986 and 1987, raises the possibility that the volume of drug-related appeals has doubled in the past few years. For this reason, future research should devote special attention to the impact of increasing efforts to prosecute drug-related offenses. Finally, although homicides constitute the smallest category of offenses on appeal, the cross-court similarity in the relative frequencies is striking. All the courts are close to the four-court average of 8 percent.

The information in Tables 3 and 4 is significant because it indicates not only that the areas of civil law and underlying offenses in civil and criminal appeals are similar across courts but that this commonality exists despite important differences in the courts' subject matter jurisdiction and in the underlying trial court proceedings. One important implication of this finding is that caseflow management principles can be developed and applied generally to IACs. If the area of law and criminal offense patterns are similar across jurisdictions, courts can follow common principles in screening and monitor-

Table 4
Underlying Offense in Decided Criminal Appeals*

	Arizona	Florida	Maryland	New Jersey
Homicide	6%	8%	11%	8%
Other Crimes Against the Person	29	34	37	36
Property	24	16	12	11
Drug Sales or Possession	16	23	16	23
Other	24	18	24	22
	n=361	n=345	n=335	n=288

*Appeals are classified according to the most serious offense at conviction.

ing appeals. This commonality among courts suggests that while reforms may have to be tailored to fit particular needs and circumstances, the caseload pressures confronting IACs are not totally unique and need not frustrate the development of systematic approaches to improving case processing.

Attrition

As seen in **Tables 5** and **6**, the four courts have different wash out rates for both civil and criminal appeals. Maryland and New Jersey use settlement conferences to promote civil case attrition before the trial court record is filed. The programs are run by sitting judges in Maryland and by retired judges in New Jersey. (In both courts, there are settlements or dismissals in about 35 to 40 percent of the cases scheduled for conference.) Although only 48 percent of the

Table 5
Attrition Rates in Civil Appeals

	Arizona	Florida	Maryland	New Jersey
Wash Out Before Record Received	NA	26%	30%	14%
Additional Wash Out by Close of Briefing	37	7	20	22
Wash Out Post-briefing	19	4	2	4
Filings Resolved by Opinion	44	63	48	60
	n=378	n=487	n=544	n=561

Table 6
Attrition Rates in Criminal Appeals

	Arizona	Florida	Maryland	New Jersey
Wash Out Before Record Received	2	3	13	3
Additional Wash Out by Close of Briefing	25	3	11	10
Wash Out Post-briefing	3	1	1	1
Filings Resolved by Opinion	70	93	75	86
	n=531	n=527	n=400	n=424

filed civil appeals are decided by the court in Maryland, and 60 percent in New Jersey, there may be substantial attrition even where no effort is made to promote settlements. Florida's attrition rate of 37 percent, without the use of a settlement conference, is almost as high as New Jersey's figure of 40 percent. Prerecord attrition information is unavailable from Arizona, but court records show that over one-third of the docketed civil appeals are settled or dismissed before the close of briefing.

There are also intercourt differences in the criminal attrition rates, although they are lower than civil attrition rates. The court decides 70 percent of the filed criminal appeals in Arizona, 75 percent in Maryland, 86 percent in New Jersey, and 93 percent in Florida.

It thus appears that appeals follow a funnel-like process that parallels trial court dynamics. The falloff is far greater in civil than in criminal appeals and occurs later in the process. These findings have separate implications for civil and for criminal appeals. For civil appeals, an appellate settlement program is not necessarily appropriate in courts with high attrition rates. Each individual appellate court should gather baseline information on its attrition rate to assess the need for and potential benefit of a settlement conference program. The higher the baseline attrition rate, the less likely it is that a settlement program will be successful in reducing the number of appeals that the court must decide on the merits. Only if the attrition rate is low should intervention in the process be considered. If the court establishes a settlement conference program, the baseline data will provide a reasonable benchmark for assessing its effects.

On the criminal side, the higher attrition rates at the briefing stage in Arizona and Maryland than in the other two courts implies a potential to reduce the volume of criminal appeals. Defense counsel, even in indigency appeals, may be able to suggest to their clients alternative avenues of relief that are likely to be more productive than the appellate process. This may facilitate the filing of briefs in the appeals that are pursued.

Blank

How Intermediate Appellate Courts Organize and Handle Their Work

How Intermediate
Appellate Courts Organize
and Handle Their Work

The traditional model of the appeals process is a sequence of a few basic steps. Beginning with transcript and record preparation, followed by written briefs, a court conference, oral argument, and a decision conference, the process ends with a published opinion. However, IACs have modified these traditional steps in important ways. Oral argument, for example, may consist of 10 minutes on a summary calendar, one hour on a regular calendar, or may have no set limits for cases on a no-briefing fast track. Because the court procedures can be expected to affect case processing, information on procedural modifications is essential. Yet, there is very little systematic information on how individual courts organize and handle their work.

The available information indicates that many courts have adopted a procedure to expedite at least some portion of their caseloads (National Center for State Courts, 1985). However, there is very little in the way of specific information concerning what these modifications look like. The alterations that IACs make cannot be assumed to be identical because these are relatively new institutions whose jurisdictional arrangements, as seen in the previous chapter, are still evolving. Moreover, because the steps in the appellate process are interrelated, it is important to know what combination of changes a court may introduce. It is important because a court can, to a great extent, determine where it wants to be fast or slow by using expedited procedures, enforcing rules, restricting the number of submissions, and so forth. The problem of determining how courts organize themselves raises several questions that the aggregate information does not reveal.

- What steps in the traditional process are modified?
- In what ways are the steps modified?
- Are those modifications expected to achieve greater productivity?

This chapter addresses these questions by describing the steps of the appeals process in the four courts. This information provides a profile of each court and puts it into comparative perspective. Are particular steps modified by all courts? Have some courts introduced more modifications than others?

Steps in the Appeals Process

What one might understand as the traditional appellate process exists, if at all, in most courts for only a small portion of appeals. The press of volume and the routine nature of many first-level appeals have led many intermediate appellate courts to reexamine the traditional process and to adopt modified procedures. The courts examined in this research are not exceptions. While what is modified, how, and for which appeals are decisions that each court makes for itself, no part of what might be understood as the traditional appellate process was unaffected in all four courts.

Transcripts

The manner in which the verbatim transcript is produced in the four courts fell into two groups, illustrating the current experimentation with alternatives to traditional stenotype reporting. Computer-aided transcription is used in the Maricopa County (Phoenix) Superior Court; there is audio recording in parts of Maryland. Elsewhere, stenotype remained the primary reporting method.

The extent to which transcript preparation was considered to be a problem is variable. Although the conventional wisdom is that transcript preparation is a serious problem everywhere, it is not always a problem for every type of case. None of the participants interviewed for this study indicated that transcription delays are a serious problem in civil appeals.

Transcripts for criminal appeals are not seen as a serious problem in Arizona, although the court spends time reviewing requests for extensions to file transcripts in many cases. In Maryland, criminal appeal transcripts are considered a serious problem only in Baltimore City (source of about one-third of the criminal appeals). Transcription is not viewed as a problem in Florida, although the long delays in briefing (see Table 8) dominate the court's concerns during the preparation phase of criminal appeals.

Not all transcript problems in criminal appeals relate solely to delay in transcription. In New Jersey, concerns over transcript preparation time are compounded by concerns over the accuracy and completeness of trial court record entries. The appellate public defender, who is responsible for ordering the transcripts, spends a considerable amount of time determining which proceedings will require transcripts. Delays arise when it is later found that all the necessary transcripts have not been ordered. This problem does not exist in Arizona and Maryland. With the majority of its criminal appeals coming from one trial court, Arizona has established a formal appeals coordinator's office in the Maricopa County Superior Court. In Maryland, the appellate defender's office, which like its counterpart in New Jersey is responsible for ordering the transcript, appears to have established cooperative relationships with the individual trial court clerks throughout the state.

Briefs

Briefing is an important indicator of the degree of case complexity. The number of briefs filed and their length are each different across the four courts. What appeared to be "natural" differences across the courts were accentuated in some cases by variations in practices and procedures.

On the civil side, appeals in Arizona and Florida have more briefs than those in Maryland and New Jersey. In New Jersey, 75 percent of the civil appeals decided on the merits have no more than two briefs. The corresponding percentage is 54 in Maryland, but only 28 and 29 percent in Arizona and Florida. That more briefs are filed does not necessarily mean that the total number of pages is greater. There is very little difference in the median length of the total brief pages that are filed. It ranged across three courts (page lengths were unavailable in New Jersey) from 20 to 22 pages for the appellant and 14 to 18 pages for the appellee.

The picture is somewhat different on the criminal side, where, if measured by the number of briefs and total pages filed, the caseload is less complex. Most criminal appeals have no more than two briefs. The respective percentages of criminal appeals having no more than two briefs for Florida, Arizona, Maryland, and New Jersey are 74, 83, 90, and 96. Median brief lengths range from 4 to 11 pages for appellants and 7 to 9 pages for appellees. The differences between briefing patterns are accentuated by two procedural differences. In Arizona, over half of the defense appeals are presented on *Anders* briefs, and while the defendant is permitted to file a pro se supplemental brief, the government as appellee does not routinely file a brief. Briefing is eliminated in New Jersey for appeals raising only sentencing issues (one-third of all criminal appeals) (see Oral Argument, *infra*). However, New Jersey's chief judge believes that recent drug and sentencing legislation has increased the complexity of that state's criminal appeals notwithstanding the number and briefs related thereto.

Oral Argument

There are differences both across courts and within courts on the availability of oral argument and on how nonargued appeals are handled by the courts. However, the relationship between the availability of oral argument and the extent to which appeals are actually argued is not a simple one.

On the civil side, in Arizona and New Jersey, oral argument is available on request of counsel. In Florida, the court may decline a request for argument, but in practice it does not do so. In Maryland, counsel request argument, but after a review of the briefs, appeals can be placed on the summary or no-argument calendar. This is infrequently done, however.

Looking solely at the extent to which oral argument is available, one might expect the highest levels of argument in New Jersey and Arizona, followed by Florida, with the lowest in Maryland. The nearly opposite is true. The percentage of appeals that are argued as opposed to being submitted for decision without oral argument is 50 percent in New Jersey, 64 percent in Arizona, 62 percent in Florida, and 85 percent in Maryland.

On the criminal side, argument is not automatic upon request in Arizona, and the court traditionally has granted few requests for oral argument. In Maryland, summary calendaring is more common for criminal appeals than for civil appeals, but the public defender does not ask routinely for oral argument. The Florida public defender rarely asks for argument. The percentage of criminal appeals that are argued is 1 percent in Arizona, 8 percent in Florida, 34 percent in Maryland, and 49 percent in New Jersey. In New Jersey, the overall percentage of argued appeals reflects the fact that the court decides all sentencing appeals without briefs, relying only on the transcript and oral argument: Two-thirds of the oral arguments in criminal appeals are in sentencing appeals; only 25 percent of the nonsentencing criminal appeals are argued. Thus, even though the Maryland court systematically reviews appellants' requests for oral argument, the incidence of oral argument is higher than in some courts that provide it "on demand."

Conferencing

The courts also differ in how they handle appeals submitted without oral argument. These differences affect the court's conferencing and acceleration of submission for decision. In Maryland, where the month for argument or submission without argument is set after docketing, there is no advancement of submission for nonargued appeals; nonargued appeals are not conferenced in person. In Florida, nonargued appeals are calendared separately for a conference session (up to 15 appeals); these sessions are held one to two times a month depending upon the volume of ready appeals. In Arizona, the calendar for each sitting consists of a certain number of cases with and without oral argument; civil and criminal appeals have different sittings, and there are different numbers of cases on each calendar (e.g., three to four argued and one to two nonargued civil appeals on a calendar; eight to nine criminal appeals on a calendar). The result of the separate calendaring is that the time between the completion of briefing and calendaring is shorter for appeals submitted without oral argument than for appeals that are argued. The court discusses all appeals in a conference held at the conclusion of each calendar. In New Jersey, each calendar consists of a fixed ratio of argued and nonargued appeals; the result has been that ready-waived appeals are submitted in advance of argued appeals. Sentencing appeals are on a separate calendar; the number of appeals scheduled varies depending on the number of ready cases.

There is no evidence that differences in conferencing practices influence an attorney's decision to request oral argument. Taking place out of public view, the court's conferencing practices remain a subject about which most attorneys are unaware. This applies to both knowledge of what goes on in specific courts and awareness of the broader range of alternative practices. For example, judges in both Arizona and Florida remarked favorably on their courts' practice of meeting in-person to discuss appeals that are submitted without argument, a practice that is far from uniform in IACs across the country. On the other hand, attorneys practicing in those two courts, even the appellate specialists, either assumed that appeals submitted without argument received a lesser consideration or expressed surprise that appeals would be decided without such a face-to-face exploration by the judges.

Decision

Much of the concern over the decision phase in IACs is directed to publication rates because of the time that is assumed to be expended in preparing an opinion for publication. While this report cannot document judicial effort, it does provide information on two other measures of the effort the court makes at the decision phase. These measures are the form of both published and unpublished decisions and their length.

There is considerable variation in the form of the court's decision. In Arizona, Maryland, and New Jersey, the majority of the decisions contain the court's reasons for the outcome reached, but differences exist in the use of authored opinions and publication rates. In Arizona, the court uses few per curiam opinions; both published and unpublished opinions (memorandum decisions) are signed. The panel decides whether the opinion will be published and circulates the opinion to the full court only for its comments. In Maryland, decisions are by opinion and either published and signed or unpublished and unsigned (called per curiam opinions). If the panel that decides the case recommends publication, the full court must review the decision and confirm the recommendation to publish it. Decisions not recommended for publication are not reviewed by the full court before release. In New Jersey, sentencing appeals are decided by order. In other appeals, the deciding panel recommends publication to a committee of retired state supreme court justices. In Florida, the three decision options are opinion, per curiam opinions (also published though they are often short, reasoned reversals), and per curiam affirmances or PCAs (which are one-line orders). Opinions and per curiam opinions are published; per curiam affirmances are not.

The publication rates vary somewhat. In civil appeals, Arizona publishes 26 percent of its decisions, Maryland 28 percent, New Jersey 8 percent. Thirty-four percent of Florida's decisions are full opinions and 5 percent are per curiam opinions. In criminal appeals, Arizona publishes 3 percent, Maryland 11 percent, New Jersey 3 percent. As in civil appeals, Florida has the highest publication rate, with 25 percent written opinions and 9 percent per curiam opinions.

Opinions in civil appeals are typically longer than those in criminal appeals. Arizona writes the longest opinions: the median length of a published opinion is 12 pages for civil and 8 pages for criminal appeals. Unpublished opinions are 8 and 4 pages, respectively. In Florida, civil and criminal opinions are 5 and 3 pages, respectively. In Maryland, there is no systematic difference in length between published and unpublished opinions (9 and 6 pages for civil and criminal appeals). In New Jersey, published opinions are 9 pages for civil appeals and 7 pages for criminal appeals; unpublished opinions of both types are 4 pages. (The New Jersey figures exclude sentencing appeals, which are resolved by order.)

In summary, some modifications of the traditional appellate process have achieved a status as almost standard in themselves. The submission on the briefs without oral argument and unpublished opinions are examples of this alternative standard. In all four courts, some appeals are submitted for decision without oral argument, with the courts differing in the extent to which argument is available or encouraged. Unpublished opinions are used in all courts except Florida, but that court has modified the form of the decision in a different fashion.

Procedural Differentiation

Despite the fact that all of the courts have altered one or more of the basic steps in the appellate process, questions still remain concerning the appropriateness of procedural changes. A common concern is that modifying a step of the process (e.g., limiting briefs, restricting oral argument, writing memorandum opinions) impairs the quality of review (Bazelon, 1971; Davies, 1982). The remaining portion of this chapter is devoted to illustrating procedures that some of the four courts have designed. The examined procedures highlight the concerns over productivity and quality that are central to court reform.

Sometimes a court will create a fast-track procedure by combining modifications of several steps. New Jersey does this in its sentencing calendar: appeals raising sentencing issues require no briefs, are heard on an accelerated calendar, and are decided by order. This procedure has been designed to help the court handle its high volume of these appeals. The benefits are that the court can hear these appeals more expeditiously, and the public defender can bring the appeals without having to write briefs. The justification for this procedure is that the legal issues in sentencing challenges are settled, and questions regarding the application of law to fact can be adequately presented upon review of the transcript and in argument alone. The court also believes that quality is enhanced; by concentrating these appeals on calendars separate from other appeals, undesirable disparities in sentences can surface more clearly.

A similar idea—modifying both what the court does and what attorneys do—is seen in Maryland's expedited procedure. Unlike New Jersey's sentencing calendar, which applies to a specific category of appeals that can be objectively defined, the expedited procedure in Maryland is voluntary and can be used in any kind of appeal. The procedure involves short briefs filed in a compressed time frame and accelerated submission to the court (with or without oral argument). In contrast to the New Jersey procedure, which is seen as a way of handling a large portion of the caseload, the Maryland procedure is not seen as appropriate for a large number of appeals, and the court does not promote its use.

A different type of differentiation is seen in other procedures in New Jersey and Florida. These, on their face, involve only a single aspect of the appeal. In New Jersey, a clear majority of both civil and criminal appeals are heard by two- rather than three-judge panels. In Florida, almost two-thirds of all appeals decided on the merits have no reasoned written decision, published or not; all other appeals have a reasoned decision that is published. Neither of these modifications is a recent innovation and both are fully institutionalized. The justifications given for those procedures illustrate the policy options available to IACs and the considerations they make to meet caseload increases. They also illustrate the interrelationships among the components of the appellate process.

One of the basic assumptions about appellate review is that it is collegial— a decision of a single trial judge will not be overturned by a single judge on review, but only by a group of judges. At the intermediate appellate court level, this has come to be accepted as a panel of no fewer than three judges. Occasionally, motions or petitions for discretionary review are decided by fewer than three judges, but merits decisions are typically made by a three-judge panel. In New Jersey, however, over 60 percent of civil appeals and 80 percent of criminal appeals are made by two-judge panels.

The judges see the two-member panel as a device that increases productivity and averts a backlog of briefed appeals. Without increasing the number of appeals on which each judge sits, the use of two-judge panels automatically increases by one-third the number of appeals three judges can hear each month, thus reducing the time from the close of briefing to argument. The judges accept this modification because they believe that the court correctly identifies the appeals appropriate for two-judge panels; the quality of their consideration of each appeal is not diminished, and appeal outcomes are not affected.

The procedure works as follows. A preliminary identification of appeals appropriate for two-judge panels is made by the appellate court research staff director after a review of the record and briefs, and this designation is followed when the appeals are calendared. The presiding judge of the part to which a calendar is assigned can change the panel size for any appeal, as can the panel itself.

Although the two-judge panel has been in place in New Jersey since 1977, the technique may not be appropriate elsewhere unless other procedures are also in place. In New Jersey, the quality of appellate review is maintained by two important safeguards. First, written decisions in every appeal explain the court's reasons for the outcome. Second, the several layers of screening (experienced staff review plus scrutiny by judges) ensure that only appropriate cases are heard by two-judge panels. Finally, the two-judge panel is workable on a practical level because an appeal may be reassigned to a three-judge panel without rescheduling the date of argument.

The Florida court's use of the per curiam affirmance (PCA) also illustrates a way in which the time from argument or submission without argument to decision can be reduced in routine appeals; that is, appeals fully governed by existing law. Eliminating the requirement for a written decision with reasons enables the court to devote more time and effort to opinion writing in the more difficult or complex appeals. The judges are comfortable with this departure from the traditional process because they are satisfied that the quality of review is not diminished. Specifically, the court meets in person to discuss every appeal. This face-to-face discussion of each appeal satisfies the court of the consensus of the panel on the outcome of the appeal and the appropriateness of the PCA format for the decision.

In summary, an examination of court procedures suggests that there is no step in the traditional process that is indispensable for all appeals. Every step involves some modification by some court. Yet, despite substantial modifications, the traditional appellate process remains the procedural norm for all intermediate appellate courts. When they do depart from it, they build in other procedures to ensure that the quality of review is not compromised. One implication of this is that while problems of volume and delay drive the search for alternative ways of resolving cases, reduction in case processing time is not sufficient by itself to warrant adoption of a new procedure.

Time on Appeal

Time on Appeal

One important measure of appellate court performance is expeditious case processing. The pace of litigation is important because until the appellate process is completed, there is uncertainty concerning the validity of lower court decisions. Additionally, appellate court delay compounds problems that may have arisen as a result of trial court delay. The American Bar Association has drawn attention to this issue by establishing time standards for the processing of appeals, as it has for trial courts. Yet despite the significance of measuring and analyzing appellate court case processing, there is very little in the way of information on how well courts are doing.

The only comparative study of state appellate-court case processing, including both intermediate appellate courts and courts of last resort, was conducted 10 years ago (Martin and Prescott, 1981). One of the study's basic conclusions is that the pace of litigation is unrelated to the type of case on appeal. It is important to test that proposition against the data presented in this report because the results have important implications. If casetype is related to appeal time, then this finding provides a basis for the early screening of cases, placing them on separate procedural tracks and monitoring each track to ensure that time schedules are met (see also Whittaker, 1974; Baker, 1985). If casetype is unrelated, this encourages the use of uniform time schedules and procedures. Because these implications suggest substantially different management strategies, it is important to measure case processing time and to understand the reasons why some cases move faster than others.

This chapter addresses several interrelated questions relating to the time involved in processing appeals. Do criminal appeals take longer than civil appeals to resolve? Do differences emerge at particular stages of the appellate process? Are either the overall processing times or the times between stages similar across courts? Is variation in case processing time the product of case characteristics or the application of specific procedures? Is it significant after taking the underlying trial court proceeding into account? Alternatively, does the use of oral argument add to the length of time between the close of briefing and the date of argument or submission without oral argument?

As discussed in detail below, this research indicates that time on appeal varies along several basic dimensions. Criminal appeals take longer than civil appeals, but the difference occurs largely in briefing, particularly in the time required for filing the appellant's opening brief. Further findings challenge Martin and Prescott's conclusions. Specifically, in criminal appeals, the most serious offense at conviction emerges as a strong and consistent predictor of appeal time. In civil appeals, the underlying trial court proceeding is consistently related to time on appeal. Whether an appeal is argued does not consistently affect appeal time, but publication of the court's decision does.

Pace of All Appeals

One way of looking at appeal time is to examine the overall disposition time for a court, a measure that includes all appeals filed, not simply those the court decides after submission for decision. As shown in **Table 7**, the four courts confirm a basic conclusion drawn earlier by Martin and Prescott (1981)—that there is a considerable variation in case processing time. The average (mean) number of days from the filing of the notice of appeal to disposition in the slowest court is almost half again as long as those in the fastest court (317 to 223 days). Maryland's average disposition time was 25 percent faster than that in Florida (299 days) and just under 30 percent faster than the average disposition time in New Jersey (317 days).[9]

While the courts diverge in their average processing times, an examination of the range of processing times reveals a more complex pattern. Table 7 indicates that there are both similarities and differences in the cross-court patterns of case processing time. The similarity exists for the cases in each court that are resolved the fastest. For example, the 25 percent fastest cases in Florida and Maryland were disposed in 156 and 152 days, respectively. This consistency suggests that the amount of time required to dispose of cases that are resolved early reflects something inherent in the appeals process. The attrition of appeals—particularly civil appeals—is common to all courts, although a court may accelerate the process for some cases by using settlement conferences.

However, as Table 7 also indicates, a difference among the courts emerges at the 50th percentile and increases thereafter. Maryland, which is the faster court at the 50th percentile, becomes increasingly faster. Specifically, it is 10 percent faster than Florida and New Jersey at the 50th percentile, becomes 30 percent faster at the 75th percentile, and 40 percent faster at the 90th percentile.

Florida and New Jersey, on the other hand, which have nearly identical times at the 50th percentile (282 and 278 days) continue to have similar times at the 75th (416 and 434 days) and 90th percentiles (584 and 594 days). This pattern suggests that expeditious case processing may have a cumulative effect. A court that emerges at some point as faster than other courts becomes increasingly faster.

Table 7 also discloses a particular pattern to the time for civil and criminal appeals. In the three courts for which comparable data are available, the average time from notice of appeal to disposition for criminal appeals is longer than it is for civil appeals (46 percent, 18 percent, and 49 percent longer, respectively, in Florida, Maryland, and New Jersey). The faster pace of civil appeals is not necessarily universal, however. Arizona's average time for criminal appeals is less than Florida's and New Jersey's times for civil cases and is nearly the same as Maryland's average time for civil appeals.

Civil appeals are faster than criminal appeals at each percentile. Civil appeals are faster at the 25th percentile, reflecting their greater attrition rates.

Table 7
Case Processing Time from the Notice of Appeal to Final Disposition (Days)*

| | Percentiles | | | | |
	25th	50th	75th	90th	Mean
Arizona					
Criminal n=538	130	180	285	385	212
Florida					
Civil n=496	150	250	330	406	246
Criminal n=526	211	369	533	641	358
All Cases n=1022	156	282	416	584	299
Maryland					
Civil n=558	120	220	272	326	207
Criminal n=407	209	245	286	342	245
All cases n=965	152	237	280	335	223
New Jersey					
Civil n=565	143	251	364	474	263
Criminal n=428	234	329	561	705	392
All cases n=993	183	278	434	594	317

* Disposition appeals include those withdrawn, settled, and dismissed as well as those decided by the court.

In Maryland, although civil appeals are resolved over 40 percent faster than criminal appeals at the 25th percentile, the difference is substantially reduced to 10 percent at the 50th percentile and is halved again for appeals at the 75th and 90th percentiles. In Florida and New Jersey, however, the percentage difference between times for civil and criminal appeals remains relatively stable at the 50th, 75th, and 90th percentiles.

Stages of Appeals Decided on the Merits

Looking at the length of time from the notice of appeal to disposition for all appeals understates the time the court spends on appeals. The expectation is that case processing is longer for appeals that go the whole route. For appeals that are closed by decision, it is not only relevant to focus on the length of time from filing to disposition, but also important to look at the time consumed in key stages of the appeal. Which stage takes the most time? Is the longest stage for civil appeals the same as the one for criminal appeals? Are there similar or different patterns among the courts? These questions are addressed through an examination of case processing time at four stages: (1) the time between the filing of the notice of appeal to submission of the record; (2) the filing of the record to the close of briefing; (3) the close of briefing to argument or submission of the appeal on the briefs; and (4) the date of oral argument/ submission to the court's decision. The first two stages may be conceived of as preparation time, and the second two may be viewed as court time.

Preparation Time

As seen in Table 8, in three of the four courts, a relatively larger percentage of case processing time is consumed in preparation time than in court time for both civil and criminal appeals. However, the fact that preparation time is not uniformly longer than court time, coupled with the fact that percentages across the courts vary, suggest that procedures and court activities affect time.

Concerning the time from the filing of the notice of appeal to submission of the record in criminal appeals, Florida, Maryland, and New Jersey have almost identical median figures (65, 63, and 61 days, respectively). Arizona is considerably faster (26 days), presumably for two reasons. One reason is the use of computer-aided transcription in Maricopa County Superior Court, which provides the bulk of Arizona's appeals. The second is the high incidence of guilty pleas as the underlying trial proceeding in Arizona's caseload. Because guilty pleas involve shorter transcripts than jury trials, Arizona may be expected to be faster than the other courts. The time consumed by civil appeals at this initial stage is not much different than it is for criminal appeals. In Maryland

and New Jersey, where data are available, the median times for criminal and civil appeals are 63 versus 75 and 61 versus 52 days, respectively.

There is also cross-court similarity in the elapsed time associated with briefing. More specifically, the time from the filing of the record to the filing of the appellant's brief is longer in criminal appeals than in civil appeals. The median number of days for this stage in criminal and civil appeals in Arizona, Maryland, and New Jersey are 67 versus 34, 68 versus 43, and 125 versus 56 days, respectively. In contrast, there is very little difference in the times required for appellee's brief, either across courts or within each court between civil and criminal appeals. This information suggests that criminal appeals generally take longer to reach perfection than civil appeals and that much of this difference is attributable to the time taken by the appellant to file the opening brief.

Court Time (From the close of briefing to decision)

In the stage between the close of briefing and argument/submission, there is greater variation across the courts than between civil and criminal appeals within a court. Maryland is the fastest court, with minor differences between

Table 8
Case Processing Time by Stages* Median Number of Days

Stages	Arizona		Florida		Maryland		New Jersey	
	Civil	Criminal	Civil	Criminal	Civil	Criminal	Civil	Criminal
Notice of Appeal								
to Record	NA	26	NA	65	75	63	52	61
(n)		(350)		(331)	(262)	(298)	(287)	(320)
Record to								
Appellant's Brief	34	67	NA	186	43	68	56	125 **
(n)	(150)	(291)		(326)	(258)	(298)	(281)	(203)
Appellant Brief to								
Appellee's Brief	34	25	28	26	31	40	37	40 **
(n)	(152)	(108)	(286)	(326)	(247)	(297)	(302)	(204)
Briefing to								
Argument/Submission	191	130	107	93	47	35	95	98 **
(n)	(149)	(107)	(281)	(259)	(249)	(294)	(304)	(203)
Argument/Submission								
to Decision	63	35	16	15	29	20	23	25
(n)	(158)	(350)	(298)	(331)	(361)	(296)	(328)	(335)
Notice of Appeal								
to Decision	NA	215	285	422	268	252	308	411
(n)		(354)	(305)	(420)	(263)	(299)	(330)	(342)

 * Includes only appeals decided on the merits.
 ** Does not include appeals on the sentencing calendar. All appeals are included in the overall time on appeal.

the median number of days for civil (47) and criminal (35) appeals. There is only a minor difference between the time for civil and criminal appeals in Florida (107 versus 93 days) and New Jersey (95 versus 98 days), and these two courts overall are quite similar. The times in Arizona are the longest, with civil appeals (191 days) taking almost half again as long as criminal appeals (130 days).

Decision time, or the elapsed time between argument/submission and the court's decision, is the shortest stage for all courts except Arizona. There appears to be no major difference between civil and criminal appeals in Florida (16 versus 15 days), Maryland (29 versus 25 days), and New Jersey (23 versus 25 days). The only break from this pattern is the time consumed by civil appeals in Arizona (63 days). Thus, whereas preparation time is decidedly longer for criminal appeals than for civil appeals, court time does not fit that pattern. Courts may vary somewhat in the length of decision time, but the length of time is not necessarily any different for criminal appeals.

The overall picture of the average case processing times among the four courts is consistent with prior research by Martin and Prescott (1981). Those researchers noted that there were differences between courts, between stages of the appellate process, and between civil and criminal appeals. While the information contained in Tables 7 and 8 indicates that there also are these sorts of differences in the four courts under study, the next question is, what accounts for those differences?

Explaining Case Processing Time

The study of appellate court delay involves the search for factors that influence the pace of litigation.[10] Several questions revolve around determining why some cases move faster through the process than others. Do particular characteristics of the cases account for certain appeals taking different lengths of time to resolve than others? If so, what are these characteristics? Similarly, are procedural factors, such as whether an appeal is argued orally or submitted on the briefs, associated with differences in the speed at which appeals are disposed? If so, does oral argument affect the resolution of all types of cases or only some of them?

Determining whether and the extent to which case characteristics are related to appeal time can provide an important tool for appellate court management. If there are natural differences associated with case characteristics, this suggests the possibility of designing separate case processing tracks. For example, if the underlying trial court proceeding is strongly associated with appeal times, that factor could be used as a criterion for differentiated handling.

Alternatively, the use of some procedures may exert an influence on case processing time independent of the types of cases. For example, the decision to publish a case may result in a longer decision time regardless of the type of case. If so, the decision to publish needs to be managed carefully to avoid unnecessary delays.

The Relationship Between Case Characteristics and Appeal Time

Casetype has not been closely examined in the context of understanding case processing on appeal; in contrast to the trial level where much is made of casetype as a basis of differentiation. But at the appellate level, where there are fewer moving parts, cases are thought of generically. For example, in many courts there are no separate statistics for civil and criminal appeals in terms of time, attrition, argument, or publication. More detailed information for subcategories of civil and criminal appeals in terms of area of law or most serious offense is virtually unknown. As a result, there is no systematic evidence to answer questions concerning the effects of case characteristics on processing time.

Do appeals involving the more serious offenses take longer than other criminal appeals? Do homicide appeals take longer than appeals involving larceny charges? The intuitive answer is yes—but for reasons that may not be strictly related only to casetype. For example, appeals from homicide convictions are likely to be from jury trials, which raise more issues and are more likely to have reply briefs filed than appeals arising from other proceedings. Furthermore, jury trials mean lengthy transcripts resulting in longer transcript preparation time; longer briefing time as counsel pore over the transcript and record, researching the law and writing the brief; and a greater level of review within the institutional office involved (government as well as defense). Homicide appeals are more likely to be argued (and in many courts that means a longer time from close of briefing to submission than if argument were waived). They are more likely to result in a full written opinion even if not a published one. Thus it is important not simply to see if homicide appeals take longer, but to determine if they take longer when other factors are taken into account.

This section presents results concerning the relationship between case-related characteristics and the pace of litigation. Four criminal case characteristics are considered. They are (1) the type of the most serious offense at conviction, (2) defense representation, (3) the underlying trial court proceeding (trial versus nontrial), and (4) the complexity of briefs (two or fewer versus three or more briefs). In civil cases, the characteristics are (1) the area of law, (2) case complexity as measured by the number of briefs, and (3) the underlying trial court proceeding. An overview of the findings is as follows:

- In criminal appeals, different types of offenses have distinctly different case processing times, controlling for the underlying trial court proceeding, type of defense representation, and number of briefs.
- In civil appeals, different underlying trial court proceedings have distinctly different case processing times. The area of law, however, is not associated consistently with case processing time.

These findings are based on the application of a statistical technique called the analysis of variance. The analysis of variance is a way of determining whether particular categories of appeals have significantly different case processing times. Because every case within each category will not have the identical case processing time, there is likely to be some overlap between the categories. For example, some appeals arising from homicide convictions will have case processing times similar to some of the appeals arising from property offenses, drug offenses, and so forth. Hence, even if average times for categories are different, averages may overstate the differences when the categories are like conglomerates rather than closely knit groups.

The analysis of variance explores the extent to which a set of categories of cases is associated with case processing time by addressing the question, is the variance in case processing times between each category greater than the variance within each category? (Variance is the technical term for the degree of dispersion of cases around the arithmetic mean). If the answer is yes, then the categories are producing significantly different processing times.

In interpreting the results of the analysis of variance, attention needs to be given to two numbers produced by the technique. The first is called the F statistic. The F statistic is a quantitative measure of the degree to which different categories (e.g., homicides, property offenses, or drug offenses) have distinctively different processing times. The more closely knit the processing times within each category, the larger the F statistic.

A second number, called the significance level, serves as a benchmark to separate significant from nonsignificant F statistics. The significance level indicates the likelihood that the F statistic could have occurred by chance alone. A common rule of thumb is that categories of appeals (e.g., homicides, other crimes against the persons, or drug offenses) have significantly different case processing times when the significance level is .05 or smaller. This means that the observed relationship between the categories and case processing time could have occurred by chance alone only five times out of a hundred. *Thus, the greater the impact that a case characteristic, such as offense at conviction or the underlying trial court proceeding, has on case processing time, the larger the F statistic becomes and the smaller the significance level becomes.*

One advantage of the analysis of variance is that it allows for more than one factor to be considered in relation to the pace of litigation. In addition to the case characteristic of primary interest, other factors can be introduced. Is there a connection between a given case characteristic and the pace of litigation when other factors are taken into account? The answer to this question is determined by examining the F statistic and significance level.

Criminal Appeals

In this report, the most serious offense at conviction, which is the independent variable, is broken down into three categories—(1) homicides, (2) other crimes against the person, and (3) all other offenses. The dependent variable is case processing time, which is measured in days from the filing of the notice of appeal to disposition. The underlying trial court proceeding (trials versus nontrials), type of defense counsel (retained versus public defender), and case complexity (two or fewer versus three or more briefs) are each used separately as intervening variables. The reason for using offense as the variable of primary interest is that it exhibits a consistent pattern both for all courts combined and for each individual court. For all courts, as seen in **Table 9**, the median number of days (359) is the longest for homicide, followed by 281 days for other crimes against the person, and the shortest (260 days) for all other offenses. This same order is true for each of the four courts although their numbers are not identical to the four-court average.

When finer distinctions are made and the category of all other offenses is subdivided into such categories as property offenses, drug and weapon offenses, and other offenses, there are no consistent cross-court patterns. For example, drug and weapon offenses are the fastest in Arizona and Florida, but property offenses are the fastest in Maryland, and "other offenses" is the most expeditious category in New Jersey. The reason for these different rankings is that in all of the courts there are small differences in the case processing times for these offenses. For example, only four days in Maryland separate the median times

Table 9
Median Case Processing Time for Criminal Appeals
by Type of Offense (Days)

Offense	All Courts	Arizona	Florida	Maryland	New Jersey
Homicide	359	272	448	334	583
Other Crimes Against the Person	281	228	430	262	443
All Other Offenses	260	209	414	257	408
Property Offenses	272	218	422	239	437
Drug and Weapon Offenses	314	189	372	259	442
Other Offenses	254	216	444	243	255

for property offenses and other offenses, and only five days in New Jersey separate the median times for property offenses from those for drug and weapon offenses.

The type of criminal offense is the independent variable because none of the other factors, type of defense counsel, case complexity as measured by the number of briefs, or the underlying trial court proceeding are consistent predictors of case processing time. Do criminal appeals represented by the public defender have longer appeals than those represented by retained counsel? The short answer is no. In Arizona and Maryland, the public defender's appeals are faster than those of retained counsel. In Florida, the public defender's appeals are slower. And in New Jersey, the public defender's time (280 days) is slightly faster than retained counsel (299 days), but this is because of the expeditious sentencing calendar, which consists primarily of public defender cases.

Concerning briefs, appeals with no more than two briefs take less time than appeals with three or more briefs in Arizona, Maryland, and New Jersey, but not Florida. Finally, there is no consistency to the effect of different trial court proceedings across all the courts. Generally, appeals from jury trials have longer times than appeals from nonjury trials, motions, or other proceedings, but an exception is Arizona where appeals from other proceedings have a longer disposition time. *Thus, the analysis of variance is used to test the hypothesis that type of offense is associated with case processing time, controlling for the underlying trial court proceeding, type of defense counsel, and case complexity as measured by the number of briefs.*

The results, which are presented in **Tables 10, 11,** and **12,** confirm the hypothesis. Offense is related to case processing time in every instance where there are sufficient data to permit valid testing. The statistical results indicate three important patterns. First, homicide appeals, on average, take longer to process than appeals involving other crimes against the person, which in turn take longer to process than appeals involving all other offenses. Second, the processing times for each of three offense types are distinctively different. There is limited overlap. Third, the type of offense remains a predictor of processing time even when other factors are taken into account. For example, appeals arising from trial convictions of homicide offenses take longer than trial convictions of other crimes against the person.

Table 10
Connection Between the Type of Offense and the
Pace of Litigation (Notice of Appeal to Decision)
Controlling for the Underlying Trial Court Procedure

1986 and 1987 Appeals Decided on the Merits

	Homicide		Other Crimes Against the Person		All Other Offenses	
	Trials	Nontrials	Trials	Nontrials	Trials	Nontrials
Arizona Court of Appeal Division One						
Average Number of Days	362	216	295	202	273	195
Number of Cases (n)	(8)	(13)	(28)	(71)	(40)	(177)

F Statistic = 10.4 Significance Level = .001

Florida Second District Court of Appeal						
Average Number of Days	421	492	467	356	439	396
Number of Cases (n)	(15)	(9)	(73)	(37)	(78)	(105)

F Statistic = 2.6 Significance Level = .022

Maryland Court of Special Appeals						
Average Number of Days	338	203	262	252	261	244
Number of Cases (n)	(34)	(1)	(109)	(1)	(113)	(38)

There are too few cases in some categories to permit statistical analysis.

New Jersey Appellate Division of the Superior Court						
Average Number of Days	705	399	475	356	469	311
Number of Cases (n)	(12)	(8)	(72)	(26)	(91)	(58)

F Statistic = 9.4 Significance Level = .001

All Courts						
Average Number of Days	427	369	376	292	369	287
Number of Cases (n)	(69)	(29)	(281)	(130)	(322)	(373)

F Statistic = 16.2 Significance Level = .001

The type of criminal offense is associated with the pace of litigation, controlling for the underlying trial court procedure. While trials take longer to resolve for all types of offenses, except for homicides in Florida, offense remains significantly related to pace.

Table 11
Connection Between the Type of Criminal Offense and the Pace of Litigation (Notice of Appeal to Decision) Controlling for the Type of Appellant's Attorney*

1986 and 1987 Appeals Decided on the Merits

	Homicide		Other Crimes Against the Person		All Other Offenses	
	Retained	Public Defender	Retained	Public Defender	Retained	Public Defender
Arizona Court of Appeal Division One						
Average Number of Days	402	293	274	243	268	222
Number of Cases (n)	(6)	(9)	(23)	(64)	(63)	(144)

F Statistic = 4.764   Significance Level = .001

Florida Second District Court of Appeal						
Average Number of Days	371	584	450	488	370	461
Number of Cases (n)	(1)	(15)	(6)	(84)	(20)	(137)

There are too few cases in some categories to permit statistical analysis.

Maryland Court of Special Appeals						
Average Number of Days	303	345	257	265	262	255
Number of Cases (n)	(8)	(27)	(31)	(79)	(29)	(118)

F Statistic = 10.353   Significance Level = .001

New Jersey Appellate Division of the Superior Court						
Average Number of Days	0	613	409	443	355	446
Number of Cases (n)	(0)	(19)	(10)	(89)	(34)	(106)

There are too few cases in some categories to permit statistical analysis.

All Courts						
Average Number of Days	347	462	301	370	303	342
Number of Cases (n)	(15)	(70)	(70)	(295)	(151)	(505)

F Statistic = 9.906   Significance Level = .001

* The category of public defender includes some cases in which counsel were assigned by the court (Arizona and Florida) or were on contract to the public defender's office (Maryland and New Jersey). This involves 3, 1, 2, and 65 cases in Arizona, Florida, Maryland, and New Jersey, respectively.

The type of criminal offense is associated with the pace of litigation, controlling for type of attorney. Generally, homicides take the longest time to resolve regardless of the type of representation, and "other offenses" take the shortest regardless of representation. Hence, while appeals involving public defenders take longer than cases involving retained counsel, except in Arizona, offense remains significantly related to pace.

Table 12
Connection Between the Type of Criminal Offense and the Pace of Litigation (Notice of Appeal to Decision) Controlling for Brief Complexity (1-2 Briefs versus 3 or more)

1986 and 1987 Appeals Decided on the Merits

	Homicide		Other Crimes Against the Person		All Other Offenses	
	Routine	Complex	Routine	Complex	Routine	Complex
Arizona Court of Appeal Division One						
Average Number of Days	306	373	231	362	224	351
Number of Cases (n)	(11)	(6)	(70)	(13)	(159)	(28)
F Statistic = 13.457 Significance Level = .001						
Florida Second District Court of Appeal						
Average Number of Days	556	478	470	478	428	441
Number of Cases (n)	(13)	(8)	(72)	(28)	(144)	(43)
F Statistic = 2.24 Significance Level = .052						
Maryland Court of Special Appeals						
Average Number of Days	338	342	263	257	256	269
Number of Cases (n)	(30)	(5)	(102)	(9)	(132)	(19)
F Statistic = 9.279 Significance Level = .001						
New Jersey Appellate Division of the Superior Court						
Average Number of Days	604	1074	484	526	453	545
Number of Cases (n)	(16)	(1)	(78)	(3)	(120)	(4)
There are too few cases in some categories to permit statistical analysis.						
All Courts						
Average Number of Days	433	442	356	414	334	384
Number of Cases (n)	(70)	(20)	(322)	(53)	(555)	(94)
F Statistic = 6.872 Significance Level = .001						

The type of criminal offense is associated with the pace of litigation, controlling for brief complexity. More complex cases take longer, but the type of offense remains a significant predictor of case processing time even when complexity is taken into account.

In contrast to this pattern, none of the other three variables has consistently significant connections to case processing time. For example, when the underlying trial court proceeding is used as the independent variable and the number of briefs is introduced as a control variable, the relationship is significant in Arizona and New Jersey but not in Florida and Maryland. The lack of consistency is found regardless of which case characteristic, other than type of offense, is used as the independent variable. Thus, the type of offense is not only a significant predictor of criminal appeals processing time, but it is relatively more consistent than any other case characteristic.

Civil Appeals

The analysis of civil appeals reveals that the most consistent predictor of case processing time is the underlying trial court proceeding, not the area of law. Although the area of law in civil appeals corresponds to the type of offense in criminal appeals, it does not have a parallel effect on appeal time. The weak connection between the area of civil law and case processing time is suggested by the information contained in Table 13. Appeals in tort cases have the longest median appeal times in every court. Tort appeals take two weeks longer than the four-court median in Maryland and New Jersey, four weeks longer in Arizona and Florida. These differences are modest as seen by the fact that they range from 4 to 10 percent longer than the median. More importantly, although there is consistency across the courts in torts having the longest appeal times, the courts do not otherwise have common patterns in which areas of law are associated with faster or slower appeal times. In Maryland, domestic appeals have the second longest appeal time; in Florida, domestic and property appeals rank second. Agency appeals are slower than domestic appeals in New Jersey,

---

Table 13
Median Case Processing Time for Decided
Civil Appeals by Area of Law
Notice of Appeal to Disposition
(Record to Disposition in Arizona) (Days)

Area of Law	All Courts Combined	Arizona	Florida	Maryland	New Jersey
Property	270	354	294	267	270
Tort	302	372	315	281	326
Commercial/Contract	280	351	281	267	306
Administrative	303	322	244	256	317
Domestic	286	313	294	271	309
Other	260	341	270	253	291

with property being the fastest. Given this inconsistent pattern, the analysis of variance does not unexpectedly indicate that different areas of law have distinctly different case processing times.

The lack of a strong, consistent connection between the area of civil law occurs, moreover, for different classifications of law. If the areas are broadly defined (property and commercial, tort, and all others), **Table 14** shows that there is no significant association for any of the individual courts or for all courts combined. As seen in **Table 15**, a more refined classification (property/ commercial, tort, agency, domestic, other) has a significant association only in Florida and for all courts combined.

Instead of the area of law, the underlying trial court proceeding is associated with different case processing times in civil appeals. Appeals arising

---

Table 14
Connection Between the Area of Civil Law and
the Pace of Litigation (Notice of Appeal to Decision)

1986 and 1987 Appeals Decided on the Merits

	Property and Commercial	Tort	Agency, Domestic, and Other
Florida Second District Court of Appeal			
Average Number of Days	296	331	287
Number of Cases (n)	(107)	(64)	(122)
	F Statistic = 4.6446	Significance Level = .0103	
Maryland Court of Special Appeals			
Average Number of Days	281	283	272
Number of Cases (n)	(89)	(53)	(114)
	F Statistic = .4670	Significance Level = .6274	
New Jersey Appellate Division of the Superior Court			
Average Number of Days	322	331	313
Number of Cases (n)	(96)	(76)	(147)
	F Statistic = .3824	Significance Level = .6825	
All Courts			
Average Number of Days	300	318	293
Number of Cases (n)	(292)	(193)	(383)
	F Statistic = 3.0716	Significance Level = .0469	

The area of civil law is not associated with the pace of litigation except in Florida.

---

from jury trials have the longest median processing time (363 days), followed by bench trials (305 days), and other proceedings such as motions (285 days). The results of the analysis of variance, as seen in **Table 16**, indicate that the underlying trial court proceeding produces significant differences in case processing time when no other factors are taken into account. And the type of proceeding remains a significant predictor when case complexity is taken into account. As **Table 17** shows, appeals arising from jury trials in complex cases take longer than those from bench trials in complex cases. Thus, particular case characteristics make a difference in the processing of both civil and criminal appeals. The underlying trial court proceeding is the key determinant on the civil side, and the type of offense is the key determinant on the criminal side.

Table 15
Connection Between the Area of Civil Law and the Pace of Litigation (Notice of Appeal to Decision)

1986 and 1987 Appeals Decided on the Merits

	Property and Commercial	Tort	Agency	Domestic	Other
Florida Second District Court of Appeal					
Average Number of Days	296	331	254	300	280
Number of Cases (n)	(107)	(64)	(19)	(72)	(31)
F Statistic = 3.3	Significance Level = .0114				
Maryland Court of Special Appeals					
Average Number of Days	281	283	283	283	278
Number of Cases (n)	(89)	(53)	(38)	(49)	(27)
F Statistic = 1.8359	Significance Level = .1224				
New Jersey Appellate Division of the Superior Court					
Average Number of Days	322	331	322	330	272
Number of Cases (n)	(96)	(76)	(71)	(44)	(32)
F Statistic = 1.03	Significance Level = .3895				
All Courts					
Average Number of Days	299	318	299	302	264
Number of Cases (n)	(292)	(193)	(128)	(165)	(90)
F Statistic = 4.1	Significance Level = .0024				

The area of civil law is not associated with the pace of litigation except in Florida.

These findings are not consistent with those of Martin and Prescott (1981). In examining their case data, Martin and Prescott concluded there was no relationship between casetype and pace since the same casetype was not necessarily the fastest or slowest in every court. They saw this as a good thing because it suggested that no type of appeal was inherently the slowest. This meant to them that delay (or simply long appeal times) is not inevitable. However, those researchers may have taken too limited a view of casetype and its possible effects on pace. One interpretation of the fact that no casetype is the

Table 16
Connection Between the Underlying
Civil Trial Court Proceeding and Case Processing Time
(Notice of Appeal to Decision)

1986 and 1987 Appeals Decided on the Merits

	Jury Trial	Bench Trials	Other Proceedings (e.g., Summary Judgment Motions, Motions to Dismiss)
Florida Second District Court of Appeal			
Average Number of Days	351	310	280
Number of Cases (n)	(28)	(126)	(139)
F Statistic = 8.3034 Significance Level = .0003			
Maryland Court of Special Appeals			
Average Number of Days	335	276	269
Number of Cases (n)	(26)	(106)	(109)
F Statistic = 5.9 Significance Level = .0027			
New Jersey Appellate Division of the Superior Court			
Average Number of Days	392	325	302
Number of Cases (n)	(36)	(126)	(149)
F Statistic = 6.29 Significance Level = .0021			
All Courts			
Average Number of Days	363	305	285
Number of Cases (n)	(90)	(358)	(397)
F Statistic = 18.8577 Significance Level = .0001			

The underlying civil trial court procedure is associated with the pace of litigation in all courts. Jury trials take longer than bench trials, which, in turn, take longer than appeals arising from motions. The relationship holds true for each court separately and all of the courts combined.

fastest or slowest across courts is that long appeal times are not inevitable. But the speed may be the result of what the court does with the appeal, or it may be the result of its jurisdiction.

This has implications for improving case processing times. A court that has slow appeal times for agency cases, for example, might look to another court that resolves them more expeditiously in comparison with other categories of civil appeals. Is the difference what the court does? If so, this might lead the slow court to consider modifications in its procedures. Or is the difference in the kinds of agencies from which the appeals are taken or in the appeal route?

Table 17
Connection Between the Underlying Civil Trial Court Proceeding and the Pace of Litigation (Notice of Appeal to Decision) Controlling for Brief Complexity (1-2 Briefs versus 3 or More)

1986 and 1987 Appeals Decided on the Merits

	Jury Trials		Bench Trials		Other Proceedings (e.g., Motions)	
	Routine	Complex	Routine	Complex	Routine	Complex
Florida Second District Court of Appeal						
Average Number of Days	418	346	298	316	270	284
Number of Cases (n)	(3)	(24)	(46)	(80)	(32)	(104)

F Statistic = 3.892   Significance Level = .002

	Routine	Complex	Routine	Complex	Routine	Complex
Maryland Court of Special Appeals						
Average Number of Days	327	376	269	286	259	280
Number of Cases (n)	(17)	(8)	(67)	(39)	(61)	(48)

F Statistic = 4.72   Significance Level = .001

	Routine	Complex	Routine	Complex	Routine	Complex
New Jersey Appellate Division of the Superior Court						
Average Number of Days	387	402	319	334	304	327
Number of Cases (n)	(25)	(11)	(91)	(33)	(106)	(37)

F Statistic = 2.377   Significance Level = .039

	Routine	Complex	Routine	Complex	Routine	Complex
All Courts						
Average Number of Days	366	366	298	313	285	291
Number of Cases (n)	(45)	(43)	(204)	(152)	(199)	(189)

F Statistic = 7.919   Significance Level = .001

The underlying civil trial court procedure is associated with the pace of litigation, controlling for brief complexity, in each court and all courts combined.

If this is where the differences lie, an appropriate response may be to reexamine the jurisdictional arrangements associated with more expeditious processing of appeals. The relationship between casetype and appeal time indicates the existence of readily identifiable, case-related bases for placing appeals on different tracks in order to allocate the court's resources proportionately to particular categories of cases.

Procedural Factors and Case Processing Time

This section presents results concerning the relationship between procedural factors and pace. Does it make a difference in processing time whether an appeal is argued or submitted on the briefs? Are published cases associated with longer decision times than nonpublished cases? Is there a connection between the affirmance or nonaffirmance of a case and how long it takes to reach a decision? An overview of the results is as follows:

- In civil appeals, whether a case is argued or submitted without argument does not consistently affect the time from the end of briefing to argument or submission or decision time.
- In civil appeals, publication generally affects decision time for cases, controlling for areas of law, trial court proceeding, and case complexity.
- In criminal appeals, whether a case is argued or submitted without argument does not consistently affect the time from the end of briefing to argument. Furthermore, whether a case is argued or submitted does not consistently affect decision time.
- In criminal appeals, publication affects decision time when controlling for defense representation, underlying trial court proceeding, and case complexity.

Case processing time is not only a function of the nature of the cases. Courts can affect appeal time by what they do and do not do in establishing procedures and enforcing time deadlines. This section considers two important procedural factors: the use of oral argument versus submission on the briefs alone; and the decision to publish or not to publish an opinion. Do either of these factors cause appeals to move faster or slower? Obviously, there are plausible reasons for predicting that either factor may add to or reduce case processing time. The aim of this section is to test those ideas by examining the effects of the two factors. However, unlike case characteristics, procedural factors are expected to have their effect at particular stages of the appellate process. For example, if appeals are argued rather than submitted on the briefs, then this should affect the length of time from the end of briefing to argument/submission. And if opinions are published rather than unpublished, then this should affect the length of time from argument/submission to decision.

Considering the first procedural factor, the length of time between the close of briefing to argument/submission is different across the four courts as seen in Table 8. The median number of days from briefing to submission/argument in civil appeals ranges from 47 days in Maryland to 191 days in Arizona. For criminal appeals, the intercourt differences extend from 35 days in Maryland to 130 days in Arizona. However, the results of the analysis of variance indicate that, within each court, argued appeals have similar processing times as submitted appeals. The statistical analysis indicates that if a court is fast at this stage, it is fast for both argued and submitted appeals. Conversely, if a court is slow at this stage, it is slow for both argued and submitted appeals.

Considering the second procedural factor, the statistical results indicate that the court's decision to publish an opinion significantly adds to the decision time. For civil appeals, the decision to publish or not publish an opinion affects decision time in all courts, except in Maryland. Moreover, as Tables 18, 19, and 20 indicate, publication is a significant factor controlling for the area of law, case complexity, and the underlying trial court proceeding. There is a similar pattern in criminal appeals. As Tables 21, 22, 23, and 24 indicate, published opinions in criminal cases have a longer decision time controlling for the type of the most serious offense at conviction, type of defense representation, case complexity, and the underlying trial court proceeding.

In summary, appeal time varies both between courts and within a court for different categories of cases. The results of the statistical analyses of the relationships between case characteristics and procedural factors and appeal time, by revealing what *is not* as well as what *is* consistently associated with longer appeal time, offer important information for the areas in which the appeals process might be modified and how that modification might take place. Fixed case characteristics identifiable at the time of filing can be used as a basis for case differentiation. On the other hand, some procedural factors often thought to be related to longer appeal times are not, suggesting other opportunities for improving case processing on appeal.

Table 18
Connection Between Publication and Decision Time*
in Civil Appeals Controlling for the Area of Law

1986 and 1987 Appeals Decided on the Merits

	Published Opinions				Unpublished Opinions			
	Property and Commercial	Tort	Agency	Domestic and Other	Property and Commercial	Tort	Agency	Domestic and Other
Arizona Court of Appeal Division One								
Average Number of Days	97	154	113	37	74	88	61	58
Number of Cases (n)	(10)	(6)	(12)	(5)	(22)	(9)	(47)	(22)
F Statistic = 4.277 Significance Level = .001								
Florida Second District Court of Appeal								
Average Number of Days	48	85	33	41	22	18	12	14
Number of Cases (n)	(38)	(18)	(6)	(36)	(68)	(44)	(13)	(60)
F Statistic = 9.370 Significance Level = .001								
Maryland Court of Special Appeals								
Average Number of Days	49	53	56	40	37	36	63	31
Number of Cases (n)	(19)	(21)	(14)	(15)	(66)	(29)	(24)	(61)
F Statistic = 1.845 Significance Level = .079								
New Jersey Appellate Division of the Superior Court								
Average Number of Days	54	72	56	64	39	41	28	30
Number of Cases (n)	(9)	(7)	(6)	(5)	(87)	(68)	(64)	(67)
F Statistic = 2.031 Significance Level = .05								
All Courts								
Average Number of Days	56	78	70	42	37	36	43	29
Number of Cases (n)	(76)	(52)	(38)	(61)	(242)	(150)	(148)	(209)
F Statistic = 10.483 Significance Level = .001								
Interaction= 2.972 Significance Level = .031								

* Decision time is the number of days from argument/submission to the court's decision.

If a civil appeal is published, this significantly affects decision time, controlling for the area of law, in all courts except Maryland.

Table 19
Connection Between Publication and
Decision Time* in Civil Appeals Controlling for
Brief Complexity (1-2 Briefs versus 3 or More)

1986 and 1987 Appeals Decided on the Merits

	Published Opinions		Unpublished Opinions	
	Routine	Complex	Routine	Complex
Arizona Court of Appeal Division One				
Average Number of Days	87	112	55	73
Number of Cases (n)	(2)	(38)	(27)	(81)

There are categories with too few cases to permit statistical analysis.

Florida Second District Court of Appeal				
Average Number of Days	47	53	16	19
Number of Cases (n)	(25)	(76)	(53)	(136)

F Statistic = 15.974   Significance Level = .001

Maryland Court of Special Appeals				
Average Number of Days	40	58	36	42
Number of Cases (n)	(38)	(33)	(119)	(68)

F Statistic = 2.082   Significance Level = .103

New Jersey Appellate Division of the Superior Court				
Average Number of Days	55	74	34	43
Number of Cases (n)	(19)	(8)	(215)	(77)

F Statistic = 3.068   Significance Level = .028

All Courts				
Average Number of Days	47	70	34	40
Number of Cases (n)	(84)	(155)	(414)	(361)

F Statistic = 20.62   Significance Level = .001

* Decision time is the number of days from argument/submission to the court's decision.

If a civil appeal is published, then the decision time is longer, controlling for complexity of the briefs, in Florida and New Jersey but not in Maryland.

Table 20
Connection Between Publication and Decision Time* in Civil Appeals Controlling for the Underlying Trial Court Proceeding

1986 and 1987 Appeals Decided on the Merits

	Published Opinions		Unpublished Opinions	
	Trials	Nontrials	Trials	Nontrials
Arizona Court of Appeal Division One				
Average Number of Days	81	117	62	65
Number of Cases (n)	(9)	(26)	(37)	(74)
F Statistic = 6.687 Significance Level = .001				
Florida Second District Court of Appeal				
Average Number of Days	46	62	20	17
Number of Cases (n)	(60)	(40)	(88)	(98)
F Statistic = 17.133 Significance Level = .001				
Maryland Court of Special Appeals				
Average Number of Days	47	53	38	42
Number of Cases (n)	(31)	(36)	(100)	(72)
F Statistic = .981 Significance Level = .402				
New Jersey Appellate Division of the Superior Court				
Average Number of Days	78	52	37	31
Number of Cases (n)	(9)	(18)	(152)	(131)
F Statistic = 4.342 Significance Level = .005				
All Courts				
Average Number of Days	52	69	36	36
Number of Cases (n)	(109)	(120)	(377)	(375)
F Statistic = 19.207 Significance Level = .001				

* Decision time is the number of days from argument/submission to the court's decision.

If a civil appeal is published, then the decision time is longer, controlling for the underlying trial court proceeding, in all courts except Maryland.

Table 21
Connection Between Publication and Decision Time* in Criminal Appeals Controlling for the Type of Criminal Offense

1986 and 1987 Appeals Decided on the Merits

	Published Opinions			Unpublished Opinions		
	Homicide	Other Crimes Against the Person	All Other Offenses	Homicide	Other Crimes Against the Person	All Other Offenses
Arizona Court of Appeal Division One						
Average Number of Days	0	94	89	53	50	46
Number of Cases (n)	(0)	(2)	(9)	(19)	(94)	(189)

There are categories with too few cases to permit statistical analysis.

	Homicide	Other Crimes Against the Person	All Other Offenses	Homicide	Other Crimes Against the Person	All Other Offenses
Florida Second District Court of Appeal						
Average Number of Days	50	34	35	17	14	22
Number of Cases (n)	(9)	(34)	(51)	(14)	(62)	(93)

F Statistic = 8.415   Significance Level = .001

	Homicide	Other Crimes Against the Person	All Other Offenses	Homicide	Other Crimes Against the Person	All Other Offenses
Maryland Court of Special Appeals						
Average Number of Days	36	50	56	32	22	19
Number of Cases (n)	(4)	(9)	(16)	(29)	(100)	(133)

F Statistic = 11.944   Significance Level = .001

	Homicide	Other Crimes Against the Person	All Other Offenses	Homicide	Other Crimes Against the Person	All Other Offenses
New Jersey Appellate Division of the Superior Court						
Average Number of Days	0	52	64	59	16	23
Number of Cases (n)	(0)	(5)	(4)	(20)	(97)	(147)

There are categories with too few cases to permit statistical analysis.

	Homicide	Other Crimes Against the Person	All Other Offenses	Homicide	Other Crimes Against the Person	All Other Offenses
All Courts						
Average Number of Days	46	41	47	41	26	29
Number of Cases (n)	(13)	(50)	(80)	(82)	(352)	(562)

F Statistic = 6.365   Significance Level = .001

* Decision time is the number of days from the date of argument or submission to the date of the court's decision.

Publication is associated with decision time in Florida and Maryland.

Table 22
Connection Between Publication and Decision Time*
Controlling for the Type of Appellant's Attorney

1986 and 1987 Appeals Decided on the Merits

	Appeals Argued		Appeals Submitted on the Briefs	
	Retained	Public Defender	Retained	Public Defender
Arizona Court of Appeal Division One				
Average Number of Days	99	71	41	51
Number of Cases (n)	(2)	(5)	(91)	(201)

There are categories with too few cases to permit statistical analysis.

Florida Second District Court of Appeal				
Average Number of Days	33	36	19	17
Number of Cases (n)	(9)	(67)	(22)	(115)

F Statistic = 8.699   Significance Level = .001

Maryland Court of Special Appeals				
Average Number of Days	48	47	21	22
Number of Cases (n)	(14)	(17)	(57)	(207)

F Statistic = 13.73   Significance Level = .001

New Jersey Appellate Division of the Superior Court				
Average Number of Days	57	68	33	21
Number of Cases (n)	(2)	(5)	(57)	(249)

There are categories with too few cases to permit statistical analysis.

All Courts				
Average Number of Days	47	41	32	29
Number of Cases (n)	(27)	(94)	(228)	(772)

F Statistic = 4.34   Significance Level = .005

* Decision time is the number of days from the date of argument or submission to the date of the court's decision.

Publication is associated with decision time in Florida and Maryland.

Table 23
Connection Between Publication and Decision Time*
Controlling for Brief Complexity (1-2 Briefs versus 3 or More)

1986 and 1987 Appeals Decided on the Merits

	Published Opinions		Unpublished Opinions	
	Routine	Complex	Routine	Complex

Arizona Court of Appeal Division One

	Routine	Complex	Routine	Complex
Average Number of Days	48	124	46	61
Number of Cases (n)	(5)	(6)	(216)	(40)

F Statistic = 7.48   Significance Level = .001

Florida Second District Court of Appeal

	Routine	Complex	Routine	Complex
Average Number of Days	39	36	18	15
Number of Cases (n)	(63)	(32)	(121)	(43)

F Statistic = 11.455   Significance Level = .001

Maryland Court of Special Appeals

	Routine	Complex	Routine	Complex
Average Number of Days	45	69	20	35
Number of Cases (n)	(25)	(7)	(240)	(25)

F Statistic = 22.778   Significance Level = .001

New Jersey Appellate Division of the Superior Court

	Routine	Complex	Routine	Complex
Average Number of Days	64	39	29	48
Number of Cases (n)	(6)	(2)	(224)	(7)

There are categories with too few cases to permit statistical analysis.

All Courts

	Routine	Complex	Routine	Complex
Average Number of Days	44	30	31	42
Number of Cases (n)	(146)	(916)	(900)	(162)

F Statistic = 7.026   Significance Level = .001

* Decision time is the number of days from the date of argument or submission to the date of the court's decision.

Publication is associated with decision time in Arizona, Florida, and Maryland.

Table 24
Connection Between Publication and Decision Time*
Controlling for the Underlying Trial Court Proceeding

1986 and 1987 Appeals Decided on the Merits

	Published Opinions		Unpublished Opinions	
	Trials	Nontrials	Trials	Nontrials
Arizona Court of Appeal Division One				
Average Number of Days	96	86	46	46
Number of Cases (n)	(4)	(7)	(63)	(246)

F Statistic = 4.302   Significance Level = .005

Florida Second District Court of Appeal				
Average Number of Days	32	40	15	21
Number of Cases (n)	(49)	(43)	(90)	(81)

F Statistic = 15.041   Significance Level = .001

Maryland Court of Special Appeals				
Average Number of Days	46	71	22	22
Number of Cases (n)	(27)	(5)	(228)	(37)

F Statistic = 17.771   Significance Level = .001

New Jersey Appellate Division of the Superior Court				
Average Number of Days	58	58	27	21
Number of Cases (n)	(4)	(5)	(171)	(91)

F Statistic = 1.307   Significance Level = .273

All Courts				
Average Number of Days	41	50	25	35
Number of Cases (n)	(84)	(60)	(552)	(456)

F Statistic = 12.597   Significance Level = .001

* Decision time is the number of days from the date of argument or submission to the date of the court's decision.

Publication is associated with decision time in Arizona, Florida, and Maryland.

Improving Case Processing

Improving Case Processing

All IACs confront tension from the need to resolve large numbers of cases expeditiously and the need to provide attention to each individual case. This tension suggests that there are overarching issues that must be addressed and resolved by all courts in any successful effort to improve case processing.

This chapter examines these issues in two ways. First, the chapter highlights two of the key resources that courts use to influence the processing of appeals. They are management and the use of support staff. Based on the experiences of the four courts, these factors are necessary not only to an appreciation of what, why, and how successfully a particular court handles its work, but also to an understanding of what is required to transfer that success to other courts. Second, the chapter makes some final observations on the implications of the research findings for improving case processing on appeal.

Management

Three interrelated issues fall within management. Starting with the most specific, the first issue involves the methods by which a court handles its work. The second is the commitment to expeditious case processing. The third issue, and the most general, concerns leadership in the court. (These issues have their parallels at the trial court level. See, for example, Mahoney et al., 1988.)

Case Management
Courts vary in the extent of their affirmative case management. If a case management system means information on and control over the processing of every appeal from the time the notice of appeal is filed, then none of the four courts has a complete case management system. In two of the courts, Maryland

and New Jersey, however, the court uses a scheduling or docketing order as a management device, although the systems operate in different ways.

Generally, in neither Maryland nor New Jersey does the scheduling order cover the entire appeals process. The order is issued after the record is received, thus exempting record and transcript preparation. In Maryland, in fact, the notice of appeal is filed in the trial court, and the Maryland Court of Special Appeals does not even receive a copy of it in every case. The scheduling order, however, establishes briefing deadlines and the month of oral argument or submission without argument. In addition, the court operates on a term basis and does not carry appeals over.

In New Jersey, the notice of appeal is filed in the appellate division, and formal control begins at that point. Generally, a docketing order establishing briefing deadlines, but not the month of argument and submission, is entered after the record is received. However, scheduling orders covering all stages of the appeal, including record and transcript preparation, are issued in court-accelerated appeals and appeals not settled as a result of a court-initiated settlement conference. Appeals are calendared for argument or submission without oral argument only after briefing is completed.

Does the docketing order or early management make a difference? Some evidence suggests that it does. Overall, Maryland is the fastest of the four courts. One of the striking features about appeal times in Maryland is that they are more homogeneous than those of the other courts. Maryland has the smallest differences between civil and criminal appeals and within each casetype for area of law and criminal offense. The existence of relatively few differentiated procedures, a calendaring procedure that does not accelerate appeals submitted without oral argument, and what may initially be a less diverse caseload are all probable contributors to that homogeneity.

Uniform case management, rather than a variety of differentiated procedures, is the approach the court uses to move cases. This works in Maryland. The question for that court is whether increases in case filings can continue to be absorbed and handled in this fashion. Uniform case management reduces disparity in appeal times, but it may not reduce judge and attorney time (that results from differentiation). The court may have to turn to differentiation (including increased staff assistance) to meet demands for greater productivity in the future.

New Jersey at the time of this study was in a transitional phase; it is using information as a way to exert control over its workload and to reduce appeal time. By far the largest of the four courts examined, with 28 judges, New Jersey has problems of scale that the other courts do not face. It now has the mechanism in place to extend its scheduling order to include additional phases of the total appeals process. In addition, the organization of the clerk's office into case management teams facilitates supervision and provides a service to parties and attorneys.

Maryland's uniform scheduling shows that a scheduling order is related to but not dependent upon the court's receiving early information about the appeal. A scheduling order is issued, but a docketing or case information statement is not required in every appeal. Information about appeals is limited as the court requires an information sheet only in civil appeals, and that information is used solely to determine whether a prehearing settlement conference is appropriate. Maryland does not need this information because it does not differentiate. The situation is different in New Jersey, where a case information sheet must be filed with the notice of appeal in every case. This information is used to identify possible procedural deficiencies and to direct an appeal for possible differentiated handling (e.g., civil settlement conferences and criminal-sentencing calendar).

A scheduling order appears to play an important role even where it only restates the briefing times set forth in the rules. Court and counsel see the order as a statement that the rules are more than hortatory and that scheduled events will take place as planned. In Maryland, counsel view the scheduling order, which sets forth the month of argument or submission as well as the deadlines for the parties' briefs, as establishing and reinforcing the credibility of the court's scheduling.[11] Counsel see that the court keeps itself on a tight time frame and more readily accept the briefing constraints. Additionally, having the argument/submission set in advance limits the opportunity for extensions.

Commitment to Expeditious Case Processing

Based on interviews with key participants, the same degree of concern for appeal time was not expressed or demonstrated in every court either through gathering information on appeal time and reporting on it in a regular fashion or through setting standards for expeditious case processing. All of the courts pay particular attention to the time between submission and decision. In Florida, for example, where the supreme court requires that the courts of appeal report on any appeal that is pending decision in excess of 180 days, the court maintains a tickler system to alert it well in advance of the 180-day limit. In Maryland and New Jersey, the judges regularly receive information on the number of appeals they have under submission and the length of time involved.

Considerably less data are available in most of the courts on the time consumed by other key stages of the appeal. New Jersey's automated information system provides the most extensive information, giving the court regular information on the age and status of its pending caseload, in addition to more typical statistics on filings, dispositions, and method of disposition. Regular meetings of the presiding judges and the administrative presiding judge and key

administrative staff, at which these performance statistics are discussed, rein-
force the importance of overall appeal time. Without the information it
produces and uses, the court would not be able to assess performance in key
aspects of the process and to identify problem areas. A report on available
statistics is also part of the regular court meetings in Florida and Maryland.

Leadership

The four courts have two different methods of internal administration. In
Maryland and New Jersey, the court has a permanent chief or presiding judge;
in Arizona and Florida, administrative leadership changes with judges serving
one- to two-year terms.

Although the superiority of one method over the other cannot be
established in this research, one advantage of a permanent chief judge is that he
or she can provide a focus and continuity for policy development and implem-
entation. Having a permanent chief or presiding judge will not ensure the
successful adoption and introduction of procedural changes, but it can ensure
the continuity of leadership and commitment that is required where a permanent modification of established practices and behavior is involved. The chief
judges in Maryland and New Jersey saw long tenure as essential to the smooth
operation of their courts. They spoke of the time needed to understand the
administrative dimension of case processing and the dynamics of clerk's office
operations. They also spoke about the time and effort required to identify and
develop responses to case processing problems and to execute a new idea. They
saw all of this as extremely difficult to accomplish with a short tenure.

The judges in Arizona and Florida, on the other hand, favored the rotation
system as preventing factions and as increasing the level of interest and
experience across the court; they also discounted lack of a permanent chief
judge as an inhibiting factor in the innovation process. However, those with
experience as chief judge spoke about the need to become familiar with
administrative operations, the amount of administrative work involved, and
the time consumed by the budget process.

In summary, the principles of case management that have been distilled
from the trial court experience (see, e.g., Mahoney, 1988) have clear parallels in
appellate court case processing. These include exercising early and continuous
judicial control, creating the expectation that scheduled events will take place
as planned, and monitoring case processing time. Appellate courts seeking to
improve their case processing will have to develop appropriate management
models for a process that even critics of court case management at the trial level
(see Resnik, 1982) have observed is more amenable to greater judicial coordina-
tion and control.

Use of Staff

Even where there is a concern for case processing, decisions need to be made about the use of the clerk of court, staff attorneys, and law clerks. The four courts illustrate a range in the use of central staff. At one end of the spectrum are Florida and Maryland. Each have three staff attorneys who work on nondirect appeals or motions. In Maryland, the staff attorneys do not screen cases. In Florida, to the extent that time permits, a staff attorney and the clerk of court screen briefed appeals to identify routine, one-issue cases for expedited submission. At the other end of the spectrum are Arizona and New Jersey, both of which have large ratios of staff members to judges (12 to 12 and 20 to 28, respectively). The organization of the attorney staffs and what they do differ, however. In Arizona, staff members specialize in civil or criminal appeals; there is no formal specialization in New Jersey. In both courts, staff attorneys screen briefed appeals and prepare draft opinions (Arizona) or memoranda (New Jersey) in appeals of at least moderate complexity.

Does using staff attorneys affect case processing? Staff attorneys conducting research and drafting memoranda or opinions potentially increase a court's productivity. Judges and their elbow clerks are free to spend more time on the less routine cases. The use of central staff does not necessarily speed appeal time, however, and among the four courts there is no direct and obvious relationship between the number and use of central staff attorneys and time. Maryland, with no central staff, is the fastest of the four courts.

Central staff assistance seems essential, however, if a court differentiates the processing of appeals. While each court may reach different decisions regarding what procedural modifications are appropriate, few courts conclude that judge-conducted screening is cost-effective. Florida, at the time of this study, illustrates the interrelationship between differentiation and screening as the court considers possible case differentiation, the time consumed by screening, and the extent to which it wants to use staff attorneys to undertake that screening.[12]

Improving Case Processing

This research uses the experiences of four courts and analyzes the problems faced by intermediate appellate courts. This concluding section offers some final observations on the research findings and their implications for the effort to improve case processing.

The Importance of Court Context

Despite their common purpose and function, IACs differ in their subject matter jurisdiction. This contributes to variations in their caseload composition, affecting the extent to which filed appeals ultimately reach the court for decision and how those appeals are handled. They also play a key role in understanding whether a proposed new procedure will be appropriate or why an existing one works particularly well. At a minimum, this diversity implies the importance of knowing the context surrounding measures of case processing. For example, because cases vary in their complexity and the demands they make on the court, the relationship between caseload and case processing is complex. A high volume of appeals in one court may be less burdensome than a smaller volume of appeals in a second court if the high volume filings are susceptible to accelerated or modified handling.

Organizing the Appeals Process

Although IACs have the same basic procedures, they have introduced a variety of modifications. Virtually every aspect of appeal processing has been modified in at least one of the four courts examined. No court follows what may be identified as the traditional process for all appeals.

The experiences of Arizona, Florida, Maryland, and New Jersey clearly imply that appeals procedures are manipulable and that the traditional process can be modified and still meet concerns for quality. The use of per curiam affirmances in Florida and the two-judge panels in New Jersey suggest that a modified procedure must be examined in the context into which it has been introduced. The totality of the procedures in those courts sheds light on the viability of the proposed modification, clarifies the trade-offs that are being made, and indicate how the quality of review is safeguarded. Reducing appeal time or accumulated backlogs may not always be sufficient considerations to warrant the adoption of new procedures. Procedures must meet and satisfy concerns about quality and the desire of appellate judges to devote more time to the more complex case.

All of this implies that efforts to improve case processing need to incorporate notions of productivity. Differentiation, recognizing that different appeals have different processing needs, provides a fruitful way of examining the traditional appeals process and evaluating proposed modifications. (See also Whittaker, 1974; Baker, 1985, at p. 264). Because the objective of differentiation is to allocate judicial resources proportional to the need of each case for attention, it can contribute to greater productivity without sacrificing the quality of review. Moreover, enhanced productivity improves case processing time.

Managing Appeal Time

Although there is no single explanation for the differences in observed appeal time both across courts and within a court for different categories of cases, the statistical analyses of the relationships between case and procedural factors and appeal time shed light on the dynamics of appellate case processing and, thus, on how to improve appellate case processing. Such case characteristics as casetype and the underlying trial court proceeding are related to appeal time and, because they are fixed and identifiable at the time of filing, can provide a basis for early management and procedural differentiation. What fails to show a consistent relationship with appeal time is also important. This includes the number of briefs, often seen as a measure of complexity; this indicates that the accuracy of identifying appeals requiring more time will not necessarily be enhanced by delaying an objective screening until the close of briefing. Likewise, the lack of a consistent relationship between the time between the close of briefing and submission suggests that restricting oral argument is not a prerequisite to reducing appeal time. On the other hand, the lack of a consistent relationship between whether an appeal is argued and the time from submission to decision raises questions concerning the extent to which existing procedures accurately identify the appeals in which oral argument might be required.

Although the relationship between resources and time is not a simple one, it is clear that resource shortages are not an insurmountable problem. New Jersey offers an example. New Jersey has treated the public defender resource shortages as a management and procedural problem. Part of its response has been the establishment of the sentencing calendar, which in addition to increasing its own productivity, relieves the public defender of the burden of writing briefs in a considerable percentage of its caseload.

The Need for Information

Not all appellate courts collect case-processing time information. Other aspects of court operations, including caseload composition and characteristics, appeal attrition, and how appeals with various characteristics are handled, are rarely documented. The unavailability of this information suggests that appellate courts are limited in three basic ways from improving their performance. First, lack of information suggests that individual courts cannot identify with precision where problems exist or what opportunities for improvement are appropriate. This is particularly true with respect to information on the identification of cases that might be suitable for differentiated handling.

Second, the absence of comparative information precludes courts from assessing their own performance in relation to others. Are argument rates higher in court *A* than court *B*? Are the same kinds of appeals argued in both courts? Does a particular court write longer opinions than other courts? How much time elapses in each court from submission to decision? The lack of comparative information extends beyond time and case processing to procedures and the circumstances in which they are used. For example, although in use since 1977, New Jersey's two-judge panel operation is unfamiliar to most judges outside of the state. Few courts that write reasoned decisions in every appeal understand how the per curiam affirmance procedure operates in Florida. There is no systematic information on court procedures for handling appeals assigned counsel believe are frivolous or on the frequency of such appeals where *Anders* briefs are permitted. Having this kind of information makes procedures more comprehensible and encourages their consideration.

Finally, without detailed information on the methods the courts have adopted for case processing, it is difficult to understand the cross-court caseload and time data that do exist. For example, is a high oral argument rate the result of a fast-track procedure that provides argument in return for restrictions on briefing or the form of the opinion? Is a court's high publication rate the result of what types of decisions are considered opinions? Individual courts need detailed case processing information to document aspects of their case processing, including caseload composition and procedures, as well as time. Having this information will also support and facilitate a comparative examination of appellate-court case processing.

Notes

1. Exceptions to this arrangement include IACs in Hawaii, Idaho, Iowa, Oklahoma, and South Carolina, where appeals are filed in the COLR and reviewed after briefing. Some appeals are then transferred to the IAC.

2. In 1987, for example, state courts of last resort granted review in only 14.1 percent of the discretionary petitions filed. See National Center for State Courts, *State Court Caseload Statistics: Annual Report 1987* 10-13 (1989), for a discussion of discretionary appellate caseloads.

3. The ABA time standards do not make it clear whether the standards apply to all appeals filed or only to cases decided on the merits. Additionally, the standards do not specify if the time limits are for a particular portion of the caseload such as routine appeals or whether they apply to the entire caseload.

4. For an example of a single court study, see Christian (1971).

5. One indication of the dated nature of the prior research is its mingling of three COLRs and seven IACs. This would have been a more acceptable research design in the past when IACs were less common.

6. As a consequence of the study's short time frame, its results are a snapshot of each court, not the complete picture. The performance of each court may have improved considerably because of factors that the data are unable to capture. For example, during the study period the Florida court received additional judges, and judges were added to the Arizona court after the study period. Both situations may indicate that the study period was one of extraordinary pressure on the appellate process. Furthermore, the New Jersey court was undertaking a delay reduction effort, the results of which will not be observed in the data. Finally, as every IAC judge knows, there are constant changes in procedure, even jurisdiction. For all of these reasons, the IACs included in this study are not offered as normative models of what courts should or should not do. They are presented as useful descriptions of what IACs do. They highlight important similarities and differences in case processing. With the accumulation of information from these and future studies about these similarities and differences, IACs can explore promising ways to improve performance.

7. An *Anders* brief is the procedure used in instances when defense counsel can find no issue to bring on appeal. The attorney for the criminal defendant may indicate this situation to the court in the form of a brief and request to be relieved as counsel. If the court grants the attorney's request, it has the task of reading of the record and determining whether any reversible error exists. If the

court finds no indication of possible errors, no response from the appellee is required and the appeal is denied. However, the court may ask for full written briefs if it believes that error exists. This procedure arose out of the U.S. Supreme Court decision in *Anders v. California* (1967). Although the U.S. Supreme Court has approved this procedure, there is no systematic information on the extent to which it is used across the country.

8. Earlier research also found sentencing issues to be an appreciable portion of court dockets. Hanson and Chapper (1988) point out that in the California Third District Court of Appeal in Sacramento over 25 percent of the appeals raised only sentencing issues.

9. Cross-court similarities and differences cannot be examined for all courts in all respects because of limitations to the data. In Arizona, the date of the filing of the notice of appeal in civil cases is not available because the appellate court's information begins with the filing of the record. In Florida, the time from the record to the receipt of the appellant's brief is not available for civil appeals. Whereas the record precedes the briefs in most courts, the sequence in Florida is for the record to be filed after the expiration of time allowed for briefing. Finally, because the data in this report are based on samples of cases, it is possible that they do not describe perfectly each court's total caseload. These limitations are reflected in the tables contained in this chapter.

10. The factors that have been examined are primarily at the macro level and focus on structural and behavioral characteristics of courts. Research has shown that case processing is a product of how courts manage their dockets. However, as Krystek and Neubauer (n.d.) point out, the role of case characteristics and procedural factors has not been examined in detail. Because the degree to which these factors are related to case processing has important implications for how appellate courts are managed, this section seeks to help fill that void by focusing on the effects of these two factors.

11. All courts expressed themselves as stringent on granting briefing extensions, though. There is a relationship as well between rules and practice. As did previous research by Martin and Prescott (1981), this study found a positive relationship between the time provided in the court rules for record preparation and briefing and the actual time for those activities. The longer the time permitted by rule, the longer the time that will be consumed.

12. Arizona and New Jersey, the two staff-intensive courts, use different methods to ensure against a "hidden judiciary." In New Jersey, central research attorneys prepare memoranda for the judges, not draft opinions, although a courtwide word-processing network facilitates the judges' use of the memoranda. In Arizona, the staff attorneys prepare draft opinions. The court gets a full discussion of the appeal because, in a relatively unusual practice, the central

staff attorney and the law clerks of the participating judges all attend the conference on the appeal. In Florida, the senior law clerks also attend the case conference. Interviews suggest that the bar does not have a good sense of what central staff attorneys do. In New Jersey, where judges pride themselves on drafting all opinions, it is apparent from discussions with attorneys that even appellate specialists assume that staff draft opinions. Attorneys in Florida, however, expressed surprise that staff would be used in such a fashion. In all sites, attorneys who had served as law clerks generally were less concerned with staff drafting than those without such experience.

References

Thomas E. Baker (1985), "A Compendium of Proposals to Reform the United States Courts of Appeals," 37 *University of Florida Law Review* 225.

Lawrence Baum (1977), "Policy Goals in Judicial Gatekeeping: A Proximity Model of Discretionary Jurisdiction," 21 *American Journal of Political Science* 13.

David Bazelon (1971), "New Gods for Old: 'Efficient' Courts in a Democratic Society," 46 *New York University Law Review* 653.

Paul D. Carrington, Daniel Meador, and Maurice Rosenberg (1976), *Justice on Appeal*. St. Paul, MN: West Publishing Co.

Joy A. Chapper and Roger A. Hanson (1983), "Expedited Procedures for Appellate Courts: Evidence from California's Third District Court of Appeal," 42 *Maryland Law Review* 696.

_____ (1988), "Managing the Criminal Appeals Process," 12 *State Court Journal* 4 (Summer).

_____ (1989), *Understanding Reversible Error in Criminal Appeals*. Williamsburg, VA: National Center for State Courts.

Winslow Christian (1971), "Delay in Criminal Appeals: A Functional Analysis of One Court," 23 *Stanford Law Review* 676.

Thomas W. Davies (1981), "Gresham's Law Revisited: Expedited Processing Techniques and the Allocation of Appellate Resources," 6 *Justice System Journal* 372.

_____ (1982), "Affirmed: A Study of Criminal Appeals and Decisionmaking Norms in a California Court of Appeals," 82 *American Bar Foundation Research Journal* 543.

Charles G. Douglas (1985), "Innovative Appellate Court Processing: New Hampshire's Experience with Summary Affirmance," 69 *Judicature* 147.

Victor E. Flango and Mary E. Elsner (1983), "Advance Report: The Latest State Court Caseload Data," 7 *State Court Journal* 16 (Winter).

Roger A. Hanson and Joy A. Chapper (1988), "What Does Sentencing Reform do to Criminal Appeals?" 72 *Judicature* 50.

_____ (1989), "Organizing the Criminal Appeals Process," 72 *Judicature* 239.

Robert A. Kagan et al. (1978), "The Evolution of State Supreme Courts," 76 *Michigan Law Review* 961.

Dennis Krystek and David Neubauer (n.d.), "Civil Courts and the Delivery of Speedy Justice: The Influence of Case, Litigant and Processing Characteristics," University of New Orleans, Political Science Department.

Barry Mahoney et al. (1988), *Changing Times in Trial Courts*. Williamsburg, VA: National Center for State Courts.

John A. Martin and Elizabeth A. Prescott (1981), *Appellate Court Delay: Structural Responses to the Problems of Volume and Delay*. Williamsburg, VA: National Center for State Courts.

Thomas B. Marvell and Sue A. Lindgren (1985), *The Growth of Appeals*. Washington, DC: Bureau of Justice Statistics.

National Center for State Courts (1985), *1984 State Appellate Court Jurisdiction Guide for Statistical Reporting*. Williamsburg, VA: National Center for State Courts.

_____ (1989), *State Court Caseload Statistics: Annual Report 1987*. Williamsburg, VA: National Center for State Courts.

_____ (1990), *State Court Caseload Statistics: Annual Report 1988*. Williamsburg, VA: National Center for State Courts.

Lynae K. E. Olson and Joy A. Chapper (1983), "Screening and Tracking Criminal Appeals: The Rhode Island Experience," 8 *Justice System Journal* 20.

President's Commission on Law Enforcement and the Administration of Justice (1967), *The Challenge of Crime in a Free Society*. Washington, DC: Government Printing Office.

Judith Resnik (1982), "Managerial Judges," 96 *Harvard Law Review* 374.

John A. Stookey (1982), "Creating an Intermediate Court of Appeals: Workload and Policymaking Consequences," in *The Analysis of Judicial Reform* (Philip Dubois ed.). Lexington, MA: Lexington Books.

Robert S. Thompson (1987), "Visibility and Status for Appellate Staff Attorneys: A Proposal," Paper presented at the Annual Conference of Appellate Staff Attorneys, Charleston, South Carolina.

Stephen L. Wasby (1987), "The Study of Appellate Court Administration: The State of the Enterprise," 12 *Justice System Journal* 119.

David Wasserman (1988), *A Sword for the Convicted: Representing Indigent Defendants on Appeal.* New York: NYU Center for Research in Crime and Justice.

William L. Whittaker (1974), "Differentiated Case Management in the United States Courts of Appeals," 63 *Federal Rules Decisions* 453.

John T. Wold (1978), "Going Through the Motions: The Monotony of Appellate Court Decision Making," 62 *Judicature* 58.

John T. Wold and Greg A. Caldeira (1980), "Perceptions of 'Routine' Decision-Making in Five California Courts of Appeal," 13 *Polity* 334.

Appendices

Appendix I

Arizona Court of Appeals, Division One (Phoenix)

Setting

The Arizona Court of Appeals, Division One, in Phoenix (COA) is one of two geographic districts of the state's intermediate appellate court. The court sits exclusively in Phoenix. It was a 12-judge court in 1986 and 1987; 3 more judges have since been authorized. A chief judge is elected by the court for a one-year term, with possible retention for a second year. The 12 judges are divided into four three-member departments. Each department has a presiding judge and an acting presiding judge. The department membership rotates every four months. Case filings increased during 1986-1987. Overall filings increased 30 percent between 1984 and 1987. Criminal appeals increased 44 percent over this time period, general civil appeals 7 percent.

Jurisdiction

The court's jurisdiction is virtually all mandatory; it hears appeals of right from the superior court and reviews decisions of the industrial commission and the department of revenue. Unemployment board cases are the only discretionary appeals. Death penalty appeals go directly from the trial court to the state supreme court. The COA has been receiving new jurisdiction as the state supreme court has been relieved of much of its mandatory jurisdiction. For example, 1986 was the first year that the COA assumed an increased jurisdiction over interlocutory appeals.

Nonjudge Players: Law Clerks, Clerk's Office, and Central Staff

Each judge has two law clerks. The clerk's office has a total staff of 18. The deputy clerks have functional assignments. There is a central staff of 12 that prepares draft opinions in criminal and civil appeals of middle-range complexity. Support staffing follows from the number of judges. With every three judges (increases are made in threes), the court gets six law clerks, three secretaries, three staff attorneys, two staff secretaries, and three deputy clerks.

Bar

There is an identifiable civil appellate bar. On the criminal side, there is a public defender in Maricopa County (which generates about three-quarters of the criminal appeals); the other counties contract for indigent representation.

Appeals Procedure

The notice of appeal (NOA) is filed in the trial court. The rules provide for the preparation of the record within 45 days from the NOA, the transcript in an additional 20 days. Briefing time frames are 30-30-15. The court maintains separate dockets of major categories of appeals (e.g., civil, criminal, juvenile, industrial commission); civil and criminal appeals are also presented to the court on separate calendars. Civil appeals are not docketed until the record is filed; criminal appeals are docketed with the NOA.

The court hears arguments in a continuous term (except from mid-June through August). Appeals are considered at-issue when the reply brief is in (or time has expired). At the first of each month, an at-issue list is written for civil appeals (or, since there is a backlog of appeals at-issue, the appeals coming at-issue during the month are added to the list). The court schedules argument upon counsel's request in civil appeals; in criminal appeals, the court reviews counsel's request. Each panel sits on one calendar a week. A civil panel calendar consists of three to four argument cases and one to two conference (submitted) cases. A criminal calendar is eight to nine conferenced appeals.

The court writes a reasoned decision in every appeal. The decision may be published or unpublished; there are few per curiam (i.e., unsigned and memorandum) opinions.

The appeals process in Phoenix has two distinguishing features. The first is that the court transfers a large number of fully briefed, private-party civil appeals to the other court of appeals in Tucson. This is done for one of two reasons: (a) the appeal is one in which a judge or a staff attorney had participated as a party, or (b) the backlog must be relieved. With regard to the latter reason, what gets transferred depends in part on how far attorneys are from Tucson. Transferred cases are considered closed at time of transfer. The second distinguishing feature is the frequency of *Anders* appeals—over half of all criminal appeals. The procedure calls for counsel to prepare an opening brief and a motion to allow pro se supplemental, which is granted by a form order. All *Anders* appeals are reviewed by the chief judge, who assigns them to a department. Law clerks work with the assigned judge; there is no central staff assistance on *Anders* appeals. The court uses memorandum decisions in these appeals.

The court has initiated few differentiated procedures. There was no docketing statement for appeals and no prehearing settlement conference for civil appeals. There is no screening of civil or criminal cases by the clerk's office or central staff at time of filing. There is a postbriefing screening/weighting by central staff, which is used by the clerk's office in setting the calendars.

Certain categories of appeals are differentiated by appeal requirements. For example, appeals from the denial of postconviction relief come up on the original petition and record; no briefs are filed. Appeals in juvenile cases are filed in the trial court with a supporting memorandum. The trial court holds the appeal for a response from the government then forwards the appeal to the COA. If staff review determines that supplemental briefing is not required, the appeal is assigned to a department.

Management Orientation

The court does not have formal time standards. The major monitoring is of appeals pending decision after submission. Internal policy is that opinions are to be out within 150 days from assignment. A list of cases pending beyond the 150-day limit is circulated.

The chief judge rotates by election. The term was recently increased from one year to two primarily because the longer period was needed for continuity during the budget process.

Appeal Filings and Attrition

Because the court uses a different starting point for civil (record) and criminal (NOA) appeals, it was not possible to compare the time consumed by record preparation in civil and criminal appeals. However, in 1986 and 1987, criminal filings far exceeded civil filings: 59 to 41 percent. Civil appeals had a higher attrition rate than criminal appeals through briefing. The predominance of criminal cases in the appeals ultimately heard by the court is reinforced by the transfer of fully briefed civil appeals to the court in Tucson. As a result, civil appeals constituted only 31 percent of the appeals disposed by opinion.

Table I-1a
Breakdown of Case Filings (Percentages)

	Civil	Criminal
Records Received	41	59
Appeals Resolved by Opinion	31	69

Another way of looking at the attrition of appeals is in terms of the percentage of appeals filed in each category that the court must decide after argument or submission. Although the court did not encourage attrition with a settlement conference procedure, one-third of the civil cases in which a record was filed were settled or dismissed by the end of briefing. The transfer of appeals is reflected in the dispositions post-briefing. There was a sizable attrition in criminal appeals during briefing.

Table I-1b
Appeal Attrition

	Civil	Criminal
Wash Out Before Record	NA	2
Additional Wash Out by Close of Briefing	34	25
Wash Out Post-briefing	19	3
Percent Filings Resolved by Opinion	44	70
Total	97%	100%

Caseload Composition—Appeals Resolved by Opinion

Civil Appeals

The transfer of private-party civil appeals affects the composition of appeals decided by the court. A large plurality of civil appeals were industrial commission and worker's compensation appeals (40 percent). Contract/commercial law appeals were 16 percent of the total, torts 11 percent, domestic relations 10 percent, property law 8 percent, and all other areas of law 13 percent.

Thus, a plurality of civil appeals were from agency hearings. Nonjury trials (23 percent) and pretrial motions (20 percent) were next in volume. As in the other courts, jury trials made up a small portion of the civil appeals (6 percent), and all other proceedings constituted 4 percent of the total.

Table I-2
Profile of Civil Appeals Resolved by Opinion

Proceeding		Area of Law	
Jury Trials	6	Contract/Commercial	16
Nonjury Trials	23	Domestic	10
Pretrial Motion	20	Tort	11
Agency Review	46	Administrative	40
Other	4	Property	8
		Other	13
Total	99%		98%

Criminal Appeals

Homicides (6 percent) and other crimes against the person (29 percent) constituted just over a third of the criminal appeals resolved by opinion, the lowest percentage of the four courts. Arizona had the highest frequency of appeals from property offenses (24 percent) of the four courts. Appeals in which drug sales or possession charges were the most serious offense at conviction made up 16 percent of the total. The remaining 24 percent involved other criminal offenses.

The court is also in sharp contrast with the other courts in the low percentage of criminal appeals arising from jury trials (18 percent). Just over half of the appeals follow from pleas of guilty (51 percent). Nonjury trials were only 3 percent of the total. Probation revocation hearings were 10 percent of the total. Appeals from all other proceedings (including postconviction relief) made up the remaining 17 percent.

Table I-3
Profile of Criminal Appeals Resolved by Opinion

Proceeding		Offense	
Jury Trials	18	Homicide	6
Nonjury Trials	3	Other Crimes v. the Person	29
Probation Revocation	10	Property	24
Guilty Pleas	51	Drug Sales or Possession	16
Other	17	Other	24
All Appeals	99%	All Appeals	99%

Appeal Processing—Briefs, Argument, Opinion Writing

Briefs

The number of briefs filed, the number of pages filed, and the number of issues raised are measures of appeal complexity. By these measures, the court's criminal caseload is overwhelmingly routine. Civil appeals, on the other hand, routinely have more than two briefs and are longer. The majority of both categories of appeals raise only a single issue.

Table I-4
Briefing in the Court

	Civil	Criminal
Percentage of Cases with 2 Briefs Only	28	83
Percentage of Cases with 3 Briefs or More	72	17
Median Length of Appellant Briefs (Pages)	20	4
Median Length of Appellee Briefs (Pages)	18	9
Percentage of Cases with 1 Issue	62	82
Percentage of Cases with 2 Issues	21	10
Percentage of Cases with 3 or More Issues	17	8

Oral Argument

Whether an appeal is argued orally can also be a measure of case complexity. Argument can affect the time from the close of briefing to argument and submission. Oral argument is held in only 20 percent of all appeals. The frequency of argument, however, varies considerably by casetype: 64 percent of the civil appeals but only 1 percent of the criminal appeals are argued.

Opinion Writing

The court's writing practices are related to both judicial effort and time from submission to decision. The court writes in virtually every appeal, although the decision may be published or unpublished. The publication rate is in line with that of the other courts; however, the Arizona court writes longer opinions. In addition, it is the only one of the four courts where more than a bare percentage or two of the decisions have separate concurrences or dissents.

Table I-5
Opinion-writing Practices

	Civil	Criminal	Combined
Median Length of Published Opinions (Pages)	12	8	11
Median Length of Unpublished Opinions (Pages)	8	4	4
Percentage of Published Opinions	34	25	29
Percentage of Dispositions with Separate Opinions	14	2	7

Appeal Times

The median time from the filing of the record to disposition in civil appeals was 237 days. The median time from the notice of appeal to disposition in criminal appeals was 180 days.

Table I-6
Median Disposition Times (Days)

	Civil	Criminal
All Appeals	237	180
Appeals Closed by Decision	342	215

The comparison of median times for each stage is shown in Table I-7.

Table I-7
Median Appeals Times by Stage of the Appeal
(Days)

	Civil	Criminal
Notice of Appeal to Record	NA	26
Record to Appellant's Brief	34	67
Appellant's Brief to Appellee's Brief	34	25
Appellee's Brief to Argument/Submission	191	130
Argument/Submission to Decision	63	35
Record to Decision	347	
Notice of Appeal to Decision		215

Several observations can be drawn from the times in Table I-7. First, the longest part of total appeal time occurs in what is called court time—the time after the receipt of the parties' briefs. Second, the longest single interval, for civil and criminal appeals alike, is the time from the close of briefing to either argument or submission without oral argument. Third, decision time is relatively long, although civil appeals take considerably longer than criminal appeals. Finally, preparation time is short in relation both to court time and to the time permitted by court rules.

Understanding Appeal Times

The court has the fastest times in areas where many other courts are troubled—record and transcript preparation and briefing. Computer-aided transcription operated by the superior court in Phoenix speeds transcript preparation. A coordinating office in the superior court also facilitates record preparation. Adequate staffing in institutional offices, particularly the public defender, enables the court to avoid what others have found to be an extremely difficult impediment to speedier appeals processing.

Nevertheless, this is a court that has had large increases in case filings in recent years. While a crash program using pro tem judges was successful in reducing a backlog of civil appeals in the period shortly before this study, problems still remain.

The court had few differentiated procedures and little affirmative case management during the period under examination. Although it indicated a concern with time and productivity, and had stable and expert staff support, the court has had little sustained attention to case processing. The short tenure of the chief judge may be a contributing factor, inhibiting the adoption and regular use of differentiated procedures.

The data may understate the problem. For example, with respect to civil appeals, the time from the close of briefing to argument or submission would be much longer if the court did not transfer almost one in four fully briefed appeals to the appeals court in Tucson. What are left are disproportionately agency appeals. With respect to criminal appeals, over half of the appeals are presented on *Anders* briefs, and very few of the remaining criminal appeals are argued. This caseload composition suggests that procedural differentiation offers a considerable opportunity for enhancing judicial productivity and reducing overall appeal time.

Appendix II

Florida Second District Court of Appeal

Setting

The Florida Second District Court of Appeal is one of five geographic districts of the state's intermediate appellate court. It was a 10-judge court in 1986 and 1987; it gained 2 judges in 1989. The court has a rotating chief judge, determined by seniority for a two-year term. The court is headquartered in Lakeland, where the clerk's office is located and where 5 judges have chambers. Seven judges have chambers in Tampa. The court's jurisdiction includes five judicial circuits embracing 14 counties. The court regularly schedules argument in Lakeland and Tampa and periodically sits in each of the judicial circuits. During the period covered by this research, total filings were increasing. Filings in 1986 were 11 percent above 1985; 1987 filings were almost 10 percent over 1986.

Jurisdiction

The court's jurisdiction is primarily mandatory. It hears appeals of right from final circuit court judgments and specified interlocutory orders and appeals from certain statewide agencies. It has discretionary jurisdiction over extraordinary writs, including common law certiorari, mandamus actions, and habeas corpus appeals. Death penalty appeals go directly from the circuit court to the state supreme court. In Florida, since April 1980, decisions of the district courts of appeal are final in most instances, with supreme court review limited primarily to constitutional issues, questions certified by the courts of appeal, and conflicts in opinions of those courts with the supreme court and one another.

Nonjudge Players: Law Clerks, Clerk's Office, and Central Staff

Each judge has two law clerks. The clerk's office has 13 individuals, including the clerk. The deputy clerks have functional assignments. The current clerk, who has been with the court since 1968, functions as its senior staff attorney as well as its day-to-day manager of operations. Judges and private attorneys acknowledged his substantive and procedural expertise and their reliance on him. In none of the other courts does the clerk fill this role. The marshall is responsible for the court building, the budget, and personnel. This frees the clerk from those tasks. The central staff of three attorneys is a relatively new arrangement. Its chief is an experienced attorney who had been an appellate public defender.

Staff functions are still evolving. The judges are determining which tasks they would like the staff to perform given its size. Currently, the attorneys work with the clerk on motions, especially those seeking postconviction relief and writs. As time and resources permit, they are screening criminal appeals for accelerated submission.

Bar

There is an identifiable appellate bar, with several firms in Tampa having appellate sections; other attorneys have extensive and specialized appellate practices. The public defender, who is elected, handles the great majority of criminal appeals. One circuit defender is designated by statute as the appellate defender for each appellate district. That individual handles the circuit's trial cases, the circuit's appeals, and indigent appeals from the other circuits. Public defenders' offices are state funded according to a formula based on appeals handled. Actual funding has not kept up with the formula, resulting in backlogs of indigent appeals pending briefing. No financial relief is possible from the counties as they are prohibited from using ad valorem taxes for state purposes.

Appeals Procedure

The notice of appeal (NOA) is filed in the circuit court. The rules provide for the preparation of the record within 50 days from the NOA. Briefing time frames are 80-20-5 in criminal appeals and 70-20-5 in civil appeals. In civil appeals, the record is not sent to the court until after the briefs are due, allowing the attorneys ready access to it. In criminal appeals, the record is sent to the court upon completion. Until two years ago, court rules gave the circuit courts and the district courts of appeal concurrent jurisdiction over time extensions for preparing records, transcripts, and briefs. The court now has exclusive jurisdiction over those requests. (Transcript preparation time is not perceived to be a significant problem.)

The court sits in a continuous term, hearing argument every month except August; separate calendars of appeals without argument ("oral argument waived" or OAW) are submitted throughout the year. Oral argument is generally available upon request in plenary appeals, but is generally not allowed in interlocutory appeals, writs, and motions. Calendars are prepared in the clerk's office after the receipt of appellee's brief. There is no case weighting. Depending on the volume of fully briefed appeals, each judge will sit on three to four 6-case oral argument calendars and one to three OAW calendars of 15 to 24 cases a month. The panels meet in person with either assigned or senior law clerks to discuss the OAW appeals. OAW appeals are summarized, and each judge receives a staff memo in advance, accompanied by an analysis prepared by a law clerk under direct supervision of the assigned judge.

The decision takes three forms: (1) opinion (signed and published); (2) per curiam opinion (PCOP, unsigned and published); and (3) per curiam affirmance (PCA), a one-word disposition. The panel decides the form of the opinion. When completed, the opinion circulates within the court, with release set for approximately 10 days later.

The court has few differentiated procedures. There was no docketing statement for appeals filed in 1986 and 1987. The court has no prehearing settlement conference for civil appeals. In 1986-1987 the court started a fast track for some OAW appeals. The clerk and senior staff attorneys review OAW criminal appeals (and recently some civil appeals) for single-issue cases that look to be clear affirmances or reversals. These appeals are submitted to separate three-judge calendars of up to 24 appeals. The assigned judge receives the briefs and record, and each judge on the panel receives a staff summary in advance.

Management Orientation

The court does not have formal time standards, but the monthly judges' conference monitors the inventory of appeals by age. The major monitoring is of appeals pending decision after submission, in part prompted by a state rule that requires a court explanation if an appeal remains under submission over 180 days. The clerk's office uses a tickler system to identify appeals well in advance of that and reports on pending appeals monthly.

The regular rotation of the chief judge results in the court having a number of members who have served as chief judge. Three current members of the court are former chief judges.

The court has an education committee, and its law clerks use a variety of training aids, including videotapes from the Florida bar as well as from sitting judges. A judge is appointed as liaison with the bar association in each circuit.

There is no single source of innovation on the court. Yet in recent years, the senior staff has evolved, motions practices have been reformed, and fast tracking has been initiated. Ideas come from within, with individual judges proposing ideas and the clerk looking at the docket. As a result, the court has codified its internal procedures and provides a periodically revised staff attorneys' manual. In recent years, the judges have sat in the other district courts of appeal, experiencing their procedures and problems.

Appeal Filings and Attrition

In 1986 and 1987 criminal filings (i.e., notices of appeals) exceeded civil filings by 52 to 48 percent. Civil appeals had a higher attrition rate than criminal appeals. As a result, civil appeals constituted only 41 percent of the docketed appeals. The attrition of civil appeals continued through briefing; civil appeals constituted less than 40 percent of the appeals disposed by opinion.

Table II-1a
Breakdown of Case Filings (Percentages)

	Civil	Criminal
Notices of Appeal	48	52
Records Received	41	59
Appeals Resolved by Opinion	38	62

Another way of looking at the attrition of appeals is in terms of the percentage of appeals filed in each category that the court must decide after argument or submission. Although the court did not encourage attrition through settlement conferences, one-third of the civil cases in which a notice of appeal was filed were settled or dismissed by the end of briefing. There was practically no attrition in criminal appeals.

Table II-1b
Appeal Attrition

	Civil	Criminal
Wash Out Before Record	26	3
Additional Wash Out by Close of Briefing	7	3
Wash Out Post-briefing	4	1
Percentage of Filings Resolved by Opinion	63	93
Total	100%	100%

Caseload Composition—Appeals Resolved by Opinion

Civil Appeals

The great majority of civil appeals arose from contract or commercial law (32 percent), domestic relations (25 percent), and torts (22 percent). The court had relatively few appeals raising administrative law questions (6 percent). Property cases were 5 percent of the appeals resolved by opinion.

The overwhelming majority of civil appeals came from nonjury trials and pretrial motions. Only 11 percent of the civil appeals were from jury trials. Agency reviews constituted 6 percent of the appeals.

Table II-2
Profile of Civil Appeals Resolved by Opinion

Proceeding		Area of Law	
Jury Trials	11	Contract/Commercial	32
Nonjury Trials	40	Domestic	25
Pretrial Motion	44	Tort	22
Agency Review	6	Administrative	6
Other	1	Property	5
		Other	11
	100%		101%

Criminal Appeals

Homicides (8 percent) and other crimes against the person (34 percent) constituted almost half of the criminal appeals resolved by opinion. Appeals in which drug sales or possession charges were the most serious offense at conviction made up almost one-quarter of the appeals. Sixteen percent of the appeals were from property crime convictions.

In sharp contrast to the pattern in civil appeals, 41 percent of the criminal appeals involved convictions by jury trial. Guilty pleas accounted for 26 percent of the appeals. Probation revocation hearings were 12 percent of the total. Appeals from nonjury trials constituted just 10 percent of the criminal appeals.

Table II-3
Profile of Criminal Appeals Resolved by Opinion

Proceeding		Offense	
Jury Trials	41	Homicide	8
Nonjury Trials	10	Other Crimes v. the Person	34
Probation Revocations	12	Property	16
Guilty Pleas	26	Drug Sales or Possession	23
Other	11	Other	18
All Appeals	100%	All Appeals	99%

Appeal Processing—Briefs, Argument, Opinion Writing

Briefs

The number of briefs filed, the number of pages filed, and the number of issues raised are measures of appeal complexity. By these measures, the court's criminal caseload is overwhelmingly routine. Civil appeals, on the other hand, are more likely to have more than two briefs and are longer. There is only a slight difference in the frequency of appeals raising multiple issues.

Table II-4
Briefing in the Court

	Civil	Criminal
Percentage of Cases with 2 Briefs Only	29	74
Percentage of Cases with 3 Briefs or More	71	26
Median Length of Appellant Briefs (Pages)	22	9
Median Length of Appellee Briefs (Pages)	14	7
Percentage of Cases with 1 Issue	58	65
Percentage of Cases with 2 Issues	24	17
Percentage of Cases with 3 or More Issues	18	18

Oral Argument

Whether an appeal is argued orally can be a measure of case complexity. Argument can affect the time from the close of briefing to argument and submission. Oral argument is held in 31 percent of all appeals. The frequency of argument, however, varies considerably by casetype: 62 percent of the civil appeals but only 8 percent of the criminal appeals are argued.

Opinion Writing

The court's writing practices are related to both judicial effort and time from submission to decision. The court publishes all reasoned decisions. (There are no unpublished opinions.) However, the court may choose not to write an opinion and to issue instead a per curiam affirmance, essentially a one-word affirmance. Per curiam opinions are used for some reversals. The per curiam affirmance (PCA) can greatly reduce the time from submission to decision: no opinion writing is required, and the decision can be released immediately. PCAs are used in almost two-thirds of all appeals, with little difference in frequency between civil and criminal appeals. The court usually writes short opinions. While separate concurrences or dissents are not common, they appear to be increasing.

Table II-5
Opinion-writing Practices

	Civil	Criminal	Combined
Median Length of Full Opinions (Pages)	5	3	4
Median Length of Per Curiam Opinions (Pages)	2	2	2
Percentage of Published Full Opinions	34	25	29
Percentage of Per Curiam Affirmances	61	66	64
Percentage Dispositions with Separate Opinions	1	1	1

Appeal Times

The median time from notice of appeal to disposition in all appeals was 282 days. Civil appeals were resolved considerably more quickly, 250 days as opposed to 369 days for criminal appeals. The faster times for all civil appeals is maintained when appeals closed by decision are examined separately. The median time for civil appeals is shorter than that for criminal appeals: 285 days to 422 days.

Table II-6
Median Disposition Times (Days)

	Civil	Criminal	Combined
All Appeals	250	369	282
Appeals Closed by Decision	285	422	372

The comparison of median times for each stage is shown in Table II-7.

Table II-7
Median Appeals Times by Stage of the Appeal (Days)

	Civil	Criminal
Notice of Appeal to Record	NA	65
Record to Appellant's Brief	NA	186
Notice of Appeal to Appellant's Brief	127	287
Appellant's Brief to Appellee's Brief	28	26
Appellee's Brief to Argument/Submission	107	93
Argument/Submission to Decision	16	15
Notice of Appeal to Decision	285	422

Several observations can be drawn from the time intervals displayed in Table II-7. First, the longest period in the appeal process is from the notice of appeal through the receipt of the appellant's brief. Second, although this is the longest period for both civil and criminal appeals, appellants' briefs are filed considerably faster in civil than in criminal appeals. Third, there is little difference between civil and criminal appeals in the times consumed by key stages after the receipt of the appellant's opening brief. While the median times required for the filing of appellee's brief exceeds the 20 days permitted by rule, those times are faster than the 30 days permitted by the rules in many other jurisdictions, reinforcing the observation that there is a relationship between the time allowed by court rules and the actual time consumed by record/transcript preparation and briefing.

Understanding Appeal Times

One of the key factors that affects appeal time is the court's use of per curiam affirmances (PCAs), essentially decisions without a written opinion, in about two-thirds of the decided appeals. PCAs reduce the decision time (the time from argument or submission without argument to decision) to a median of just over two weeks for both civil and criminal appeals. Fast decision time is not simply a product of the PCAs, however. The median time for published opinions is only 30 days for civil and 24 days for criminal appeals.

A second factor affecting the district's appeal time is the productivity of the public defender's office. The office's staffing problem is reflected in the long time consumed from the receipt of the record/transcript to appellant's brief. The median time shown of over six months actually understates the court's problem: almost 13 percent of the criminal appeals in the sample (67 appeals) were still open, virtually all of them pending appellant's brief, at the time data collection closed.

Because the court does not exert strong case management during the early stages of the appeal and shows little procedural differentiation, appeal time could be reduced with appropriate management controls and modified procedures. The fast-track procedure, which accelerates the submission of simple criminal matters, for example, might, with information gained from a docketing statement, be expanded to alter briefing requirements. The court currently enjoys an excellent relationship with the bar. This is attributable, in part, to the court's presenting frequent seminars on appellate advocacy to organized bar groups. This can be drawn upon as new procedures are explored.

Appendix III

Maryland Court of Special Appeals

Setting

The Maryland Court of Special Appeals is a 13-member court of statewide jurisdiction. The chief judge, designated by the governor, serves a 15-year term. The court sits only in Annapolis, where 4 of the judges have their chambers. Filings during the period covered by this research were relatively stable (a 6.8 percent increase between 1984 and 1987), with the increase recorded only in criminal appeals.

Jurisdiction

The court's jurisdiction is primarily mandatory. There is discretionary jurisdiction in a limited category of criminal cases—postconviction relief, guilty pleas, habeas corpus, and denial of or excessive bail. Legislation effective in 1983 removed the right of direct appeal from convictions by guilty pleas. There is no discretionary civil jurisdiction. Two categories of appeals from the circuit court go directly to the state's court of last resort, the Maryland Court of Appeals (COA): appeals in death penalty cases and appeals heard in the circuit court from lower trial court judgments, which are discretionary in the COA.

Nonjudge Players: Law Clerks, Clerk's Office, and Central Staff

Each judge has two law clerks. The clerk's office has 13 employees, including the clerk. The deputy clerks have functional assignments. There are three staff attorneys who research and prepare draft opinions on nondirect appeals; i.e., pleas, habeas corpus petitions, and postconviction relief.

Bar

Appellate specialists exist only in the criminal area. Neither institutional office is suffering from chronic staffing shortages. The public defender's office, appellate division, is responsible for all indigency appeals. That office contracts with individual attorneys in the state to handle overload and conflict cases.

Appeals Procedure

The notice of appeal (NOA) is filed in the circuit court. Appeals are not docketed until the record and transcript are filed. The court has exclusive authority to grant extensions for preparation of the lower court record and transcript. It is fairly liberal with indigency appeals, less so in civil and private criminal appeals. Stenographic transcription is the most common method, although there is some computer-aided transcription and audio recording. Only Baltimore City (the origin of a plurality of the appeals) has a chronic transcript delay problem.

The court's annual term begins in March. There is no oral argument in July and August. The actual number of days on which appeals will be heard each month and the number of cases per day depend on the attrition rate and the number of appeals submitted without argument. The last two days of an argument session are generally calendared with submitted appeals.

When the record is filed, each appeal is assigned an argument month, and the due dates for the briefs are set (40 days from record for appellant, 30 days thereafter for appellee). Counsel are notified of the due dates, the month of argument, and the possible argument days within the month. Assignment to a month is done by record number. For example, records 1-180 (filed in March-plus) will be argued in September; records 181-360 will be argued in October. Appeals with records received in January and February will have shorter time frames between the end of briefing and the argument month since all appeals will be submitted by the end of June. This method of calendaring for argument limits possible extensions of briefing and keeps the court from accumulating a backlog of appeals pending argument or submission. Argument days or sessions will be added to accommodate all fully briefed appeals.

The composition of the panels, the assignment of cases to panels, and the designation of opinion responsibility are made about 45 days before the beginning of the argument month. There is no staff screening or weighting of appeals; the chief judge examines each fully briefed appeal. Judges are advised of their panel assignments and receive the briefs about one month in advance of argument.

Oral argument is generally available upon request. The court can decline to grant argument based upon review of appellant's brief. These appeals are identified as "summary calendar" appeals, although submission is not accelerated. The chief judge conducts this review as well. The judges normally sit on four argument panels a month. Each panel sits for one day, hearing seven to eight appeals.

A reasoned opinion is written in every appeal. The opinion can be signed and published or unsigned (the panel is identified, not the writer) and unpublished (per curiam opinions). Published opinions are circulated and have to be approved by the entire court. Per curiam opinions, on the other hand, are reviewed only by the chief judge before release.

Eschewing staff screening and maintaining a case management approach, which includes argument/submission, the court has few differentiated procedures. One that does exist is an expedited appeals procedure, which requires the consent of the parties to abbreviated briefing and an accelerated oral argument. The procedure is seen as a benefit to counsel; little effort is made to encourage its use.

The court uses a prerecord/prehearing conference to encourage the disposition of civil appeals. One judge reviews the information reports summarizing the case that are filed in each civil appeal and determines which will be referred for hearing by one of the other associate judges, all of whom conduct conferences, with referrals based on geography. Record and transcript preparation are suspended during this period.

About one-third of the civil appeals are sent to conference. In the 1987 term, about 30 percent of these appeals were settled or dismissed before, at, or as a result of the prehearing conference; an additional 10 percent were dismissed or remanded after the hearing; 3 percent were expedited; 1 percent had issues limited; and 55 percent showed no tangible effects.

Management Orientation

The court does not have formal time standards, but it does monitor record preparation and briefing and maintains a calendaring system that keeps time constrained. There is also internal monitoring of postsubmission appeals.

The chief judge, who is appointed to a 15-year term, is the only member of the court with administrative authority. The chief judge screens cases, monitors postsubmission appeals, and provides the primary motivation for increased judicial productivity. The chief judge has also been the source of recent innovations (e.g., the expedited appeal and the prehearing conference programs). He has been learning about programs in other courts, developing modifications appropriate for Maryland, and taking those proposals to the full court.

Appeal Filings and Attrition

In 1986 and 1987 civil filings (i.e., notices of appeals) exceeded criminal filings by 58 to 42 percent. Civil appeals had a higher attrition rate than criminal appeals and constituted only 52 percent of the docketed appeals. The attrition of civil appeals continued through briefing; criminal appeals constituted a majority of the appeals disposed by opinion.

Table III-1a
Breakdown of Case Filings (Percentages)

	Civil	Criminal
Notices of Appeal	58	42
Records Received	52	48
Appeals Resolved by Opinion	46	54

Another way of looking at the attrition of appeals is in terms of the percentage of appeals filed in each category that the court must decide after argument or submission. The high attrition rate in civil appeals, presumably enhanced by the prehearing conference procedure, results in the court considering less than half of the civil cases in which a notice of appeal was filed. The smaller attrition rate in criminal appeals results in the court hearing three-quarters of the filed criminal appeals.

Table III-1b
Appeal Attrition

	Civil	Criminal
Wash Out Before Record	30	13
Additional Wash Out by Close of Briefing	20	11
Wash Out Post-briefing	2	1
Filings Resolved by Opinion	48	75
Total	100%	100%

Caseload Composition—Appeals Resolved by Opinion

Civil Appeals
The great majority of civil appeals arose from contract or commercial law (24 percent), domestic relations (23 percent), torts (18 percent), and administra-

tive law (18 percent). Property cases were less than 10 percent of the appeals resolved by opinion.

There was a sharper distribution of underlying trial court proceedings. The large plurality of appeals (42 percent) arose from nonjury trials. Twenty-eight percent of the appeals were from pretrial motions. Twelve percent were from trial court review of agency actions. Only 11 percent of the civil appeals were from jury trials.

Table III-2
Profile of Civil Appeals Resolved by Opinion

Proceeding		Area of Law	
Jury Trials	11	Contract/Commercial	24
Nonjury Trials	42	Domestic	23
Pretrial Motion	28	Tort	18
Agency Review	12	Administrative	18
Other	6	Property	8
		Other	9
	99%		100%

Criminal Appeals

Homicides (11 percent) and other crimes against the person (37 percent) constituted almost half of the criminal appeals resolved by opinion. Appeals in which drug sales or possession charges were the most serious offense at conviction made up 16 percent of the appeals. Twelve percent of the appeals were from property crime convictions.

In sharp contrast to the pattern in civil appeals, 64 percent of the criminal appeals involved convictions by jury trial. Nonjury trials accounted for 21 percent of the appeals. Probation revocation hearings were 13 percent of the total. Appeals from guilty pleas, which are discretionary, constituted only 1 percent of the criminal appeals.

Table III-3
Profile of Criminal Appeals Resolved by Opinion

Proceeding		Offense	
Jury Trials	64	Homicide	11
Nonjury Trials	21	Other Crimes v. the Person	37
Probation Revocations	13	Property	12
Guilty Pleas	1	Drug Sales or Possession	16
Other	2	Other	24
All Appeals	101%	All Appeals	100%

Appeal Processing—Briefs, Argument, Opinion Writing

Briefs

The number of briefs filed, the number of pages filed, and the number of issues raised are measures of appeal complexity that can be reflected in appeal times. By these measures, the court's criminal caseload is overwhelmingly routine. Civil appeals, on the other hand, are more likely to have more than two briefs and are longer. Criminal appeals, however, are more likely to raise more than one issue.

Table III-4
Briefing in the Court

	Civil	Criminal
Percentage of Cases with 2 Briefs Only	54	90
Percentage of Cases with 3 Briefs or More	36	10
Median Length of Appellant Briefs (Pages)	20	11
Median Length of Appellee Briefs (Pages)	16	8
Percentage of Cases with 1 Issue	52	36
Percentage of Cases with 2 Issues	18	27
Percentage of Cases 3 or More Issues	30	30

Oral Argument

Whether an appeal is argued orally can also be a measure of case complexity. However, due to the way the court calendars appeals, argument has no effect on the time from the close of briefing to argument and submission. Although oral argument is held in 58 percent of the appeals, the frequency of argument varies by casetype: 85 percent of the civil appeals but only 34 percent of the criminal appeals are argued.

Opinion Writing

The court's writing practices are related both to judicial effort and time from submission to decision. The court writes in virtually every appeal submitted for decision. As shown in Table III-5, it writes modest-length opinions with very little difference in length between published and unpublished opinions. Less than a quarter of its opinions are published, and separate concurrences or dissents are quite uncommon.

Table III-5
Opinion-writing Practices

	Civil	Criminal	Combined
Median Length of Published Opinions (Pages)	9	6	7
Median Length of Unpublished Opinions (Pages)	8	5	6
Percentage of Published Opinions	28	11	19
Percentage of Dispositions with Separate Opinions	1	3	2

Appeal Times

The median time from notice of appeal to disposition in all appeals was 237 days. Civil appeals were resolved somewhat more quickly, 220 days as opposed to 245 days for criminal appeals. The faster times for all civil appeals are the result of their early attrition, for when appeals closed by decision are examined separately, the median time for civil appeals is modestly longer than that for criminal appeals: 268 days to 252 days.

Table III-6
Median Disposition Times (Days)

	Civil	Criminal	Combined
All Appeals	220	245	237
Appeals Closed by Decision	268	252	262

The comparison of median times for each stage is shown in Table III-7.

Table III-7
Median Appeals Times by Stage of the Appeal (Days)

	Civil	Criminal
Notice of Appeal to Record	75	63
Record to Appellant's Brief	43	68
Appellant's Brief to Appellee's Brief	31	40
Appellee's Brief to Argument/Submission	47	35
Argument/Submission to Decision	29	20
Notice of Appeal to Decision	268	252

Several observations can be drawn from the time intervals displayed in Table III-7. First, most of the total appeal time is consumed in preparing the record/transcript and the parties' briefs. A relatively small portion of total appeal time is consumed after the court has received those materials. Second, briefing times, particularly for civil appeals, indicate that few extensions for briefing are granted: the median times are close to the briefing periods set out in the court's rules. Third, decisions are handed down promptly after submission. Finally, there is relatively little difference in appeal times between civil and criminal appeals, and overall appeal times for both categories are close to the time frames set forth in the ABA standards.

Understanding Appeal Times

Strong case management and the method of calendaring for submission, which constrain both the attorneys and the court, are two procedures that contribute to the favorable overall appeal times in the court.

The chief judge closely monitors case processing time and provides innovative ideas for the court. Appointment as chief judge enables an individual with management skills and interests to devote the time and energy into developing ideas and carrying them out.

Jurisdiction plays a complicated role in understanding appeal times in this court. On the one hand, the court largely avoids appeals following guilty pleas and appeals raising sentencing issues, categories of appeals that constitute a sizable part of the criminal appeals caseload in other courts. On the other hand, the majority of criminal appeals follow trials, particularly jury trials, which raise a wider variety of issues. Maryland criminal appeals show a relatively low frequency of one-issue appeals and a relatively high incidence of appeals raising three or more issues.

Maryland has few differentiated procedures and does not use central staff support in direct appeals. "Traditional" case management and calendaring are used. The viability of this approach is enhanced because the public defender files briefs on time. Thus, while the court has not had to make trade-offs, potential exists for time reductions if the court determines that the need exists.

Appendix IV

New Jersey Superior Court, Appellate Division

Setting

The New Jersey Superior Court, Appellate Division, is a 28-member court of statewide jurisdiction. Superior court judges are assigned to the appellate division by the chief justice of the state supreme court. The court is divided into seven four-judge parts. Each part has a permanent presiding judge. The other members of the part rotate annually. It has an administrative presiding judge (APJ), also designated by the chief justice. The clerk's office and administrative staff are in Trenton. The court sits in Trenton, Newark, Morristown, and Hackensack. Judges have chambers throughout the state. During the period covered by this research, filings were relatively stable (a 7 percent increase between 1984-85 and 1987-88).

Jurisdiction

The court's jurisdiction is primarily mandatory. There is discretionary jurisdiction over interlocutory appeals. Death penalty appeals go directly from the trial court to the state supreme court. The court has the authority to grant leave to file a beyond-time appeal.

Nonjudge Players: Law Clerks, Clerk's Office, and Central Staff

The presiding judges of each part have two law clerks. Each of the other 21 judges has one law clerk. The appellate division administrator is the court's chief nonjudicial figure. Subordinate to him are the clerk's office, headed by the clerk; the central research staff, headed by a director; and (since January 1990) court-reporting services, headed by a chief. The 90-plus employee clerk's office uses a team approach to case management in the pre-at-issue stage. Essentially, upon filing, appeals are assigned to one of five teams of case managers. Each appeal is assigned to a specific case manager who oversees its perfection. Public defender appeals are assigned to a single team, which has functional assignments. There is also a seven-member staff counsel, from which each team is assigned an attorney, who handles motions and emergent applications, reviews notices of appeals and case information statements, and provides legal advice.

The central research staff (CRS) has existed since the 1970s. The staff, numbering 20 attorneys in 1986-87, prepared research memoranda in approximately 20 percent of the briefed appeals. The CRS director reviews fully briefed appeals to select appeals for staff research, to weight appeals for calendaring purposes, and to recommend panel size. In 1990 CRS increased to 27 attorneys and assumed responsibility for preparing memoranda in all but a handful of the most complex appeals.

Bar

Appellate specialists exist in both civil and criminal law. The public defender, who handles virtually all indigent criminal appeals, contracts with private attorneys for additional support and to handle conflict cases.

Appeals Procedure

The notice of appeal (NOA) is filed in the court with a copy to the trial court. Stenographic transcription is common, although there is some computer-aided transcription in the state. The lack of complete trial court docket information on hearings and assigned court reporters has hampered obtaining transcripts in a timely fashion, as it is often difficult to determine whether all required transcripts have been ordered and received. When the transcript is received, a scheduling order is entered setting the dates for briefing (45-30-10). However, for accelerated appeals and appeals not settled at a CASP conference (see infra), the scheduling order is issued before transcript preparation and sets the date for its completion. One briefing extension is permitted by consent. Oral argument is available upon request.

The court operates on a continuous term, hearing only criminal appeals and specially scheduled civil appeals from mid-June through early September. Appeals are assigned to two- and three-judge panels within each part. With the exception of the administrative presiding judge, who is relieved of some calendar responsibilities, each judge, including the presiding judges of the seven parts, sits 31 times a year during the regular term and twice during the summer term.

Appeals are calendared after the close of briefing, taking into account the CRS director's case weights and recommendations for panel size. Each calendar contains both civil and criminal appeals and generally consists of a fixed ratio of argued and nonargued appeals. Calendars, which are held weekly, vary in both the number of cases they contain and the number of judges involved in the panel. The presiding judge of each part makes the final determination of panel size. There are 16 cases in a four-judge calendar; 12 in a three-judge calendar. A four-judge calendar will normally contain no more than 4 three-judge appeals and no more than eight oral arguments. A three-judge calendar will contain no more than 3 three-judge appeals and six oral arguments. Thus, each judge will sit on 9 appeals per calendar. Judges are advised of their panel assignments and receive the briefs about one month in advance of the calendared date.

Decisions

Written decisions are required. The CRS and law clerks prepare memoranda but not draft opinions. Opinions and decisions may be published or unpublished, authored, or per curiam. A panel's decisions are not circulated to the rest of the court before release. The presiding judges review all decisions of their parts, except sentencing orders, whether they served on the panel considering the appeal or not. The publication decision is made by a publications committee consisting of two retired supreme court justices who review all decisions of the appellate division. However, the committee generally relies on the publication recommendation of the presiding judge of the part deciding the appeal.

The court has three key differentiated procedures. First, a procedure in use for over a decade involves the size of the panel hearing an appeal. The court uses two- rather than three-judge panels for the less complex appeals, a modification that increases by one-third the number of appeals three judges can hear each month without increasing the number of appeals on which each judge sits. Approximately 60 percent of the civil appeals and 80 percent of the criminal appeals were heard by two-judge panels.

Second, a procedure instituted for criminal appeals that raise only an excessive sentence claim has been expanded to include those that raise only sentencing issues. Identified early on the basis of the case information sheet, these appeals are argued without briefs to a two-judge panel that has the trial court judgment, the indictment, a copy of the original presentence investigation, and the transcript of sentencing hearing. Receipt of the transcript triggers calendaring for argument. Sentencing calendars of up to 20 appeals per judge are held every few weeks. The decision in each appeal is an order. Sentencing appeals constitute approximately one-third of the criminal caseload.

Third, there is a civil appeals settlement program (CASP), which is administered by retired judges. Eligible civil appeals, identified by the information sheet, are assigned to the participating judges largely on the basis of geography. If the CASP judge determines a specific appeal is appropriate for conferencing, a conference is set, and counsel are notified to suspend transcript preparation. If an appeal settles, the judge issues an order of dismissal. If it does not settle, the CASP judge issues a scheduling order, with a copy sent to the court reporter. Approximately two-thirds of the civil appeals are referred to the CASP judges, and about two-thirds of these are selected for conferences. About 30 percent of these appeals settle.

Interlocutory appeals, termination of parental rights, custody, and adoption appeals are on a compressed briefing schedule: 30-21-7. These appeals also receive priority for scheduling for argument.

Management Orientation

The court does not have formal time standards, but the appeals process is affirmatively managed and monitored. The clerk's office sends monthly time and clearance statistics to the administrative presiding judge and the court administrator.

The administrative presiding judge (APJ) is looked to for leadership, but other judges are involved in administrative activities. The APJ, who is also the presiding judge of one of the court's seven parts, has sole responsibility for certain motions, including motions for extensions of time and motions to file a late brief. There are regular meetings of the full court and of the parts. The APJ also meets regularly with the court administrator, the clerk, and CRS director. Individual judges have committee and liaison tasks (e.g., with the public defender, with bar associations).

Appeal Filings and Attrition

In 1986 and 1987 civil filings (i.e., notices of appeals) exceeded criminal filings by 57 to 43 percent. Civil appeals had a higher attrition rate than criminal appeals and constituted only 54 percent of the docketed appeals. The attrition of civil appeals continued through briefing, with the result that criminal appeals constituted a majority of the appeals disposed by opinion.

Table IV-1a
Breakdown of Case Filings (Percentages)

	Civil	Criminal
Notices of Appeal	57	43
Records Received	54	46
Appeals Resolved by Opinion	48	52

Another way of looking at the attrition of appeals is in terms of the percentage of appeals filed in each category that the court must decide after argument or submission. The high attrition rate in civil appeals, enhanced by the CASP procedure, results in the court having to consider only 60 percent of the civil cases in which a notice of appeal was filed. The smaller attrition rate in criminal appeals results in the court hearing the great majority of the filed criminal appeals.

Table IV-1b
Appeal Attrition

	Civil	Criminal
Wash Out Before Record	14	3
Additional Wash Out by Close of Briefing	22	10
Wash Out Post-briefing	4	1
Percentage of Filings Resolved by Opinion	60	86
Total	100%	100%

Caseload Composition—Appeals Resolved by Opinion

Civil Appeals

The great majority of civil appeals arose from contract or commercial law (26 percent), administrative law (24 percent), torts (22 percent), and domestic relations (18 percent). Property cases were only 2 percent of the appeals resolved by opinion.

There was a sharp distribution of underlying trial court proceedings. The large plurality of appeals (38 percent) arose from nonjury trials. Twenty-six percent were reviews of agency actions. Twenty-three percent of the appeals were from pretrial motions. Only 11 percent of the civil appeals were from jury trials.

Table IV-2
Profile of Civil Appeals Resolved by Opinion

Proceeding		Area of Law	
Jury Trials	11	Contract/Commercial	26
Nonjury Trials	38	Domestic	18
Pretrial Motion	23	Tort	22
Agency Review	26	Administrative	24
Other	1	Property	2
		Other	9
	100%		101%

Criminal Appeals

Homicides (8 percent) and other crimes against the person (36 percent) constituted almost half of the criminal appeals resolved by opinion. Appeals in which drug sales or possession charges were the most serious offense at conviction made up 23 percent of the appeals. Eleven percent of the appeals were from property crime convictions.

In sharp contrast to the pattern in civil appeals, 44 percent of the criminal appeals involved convictions by jury trial. Appeals from guilty pleas (23 percent) composed the second largest category. Nonjury trials accounted for 20 percent of the appeals. Probation revocation hearings were 5 percent of the total. Appeals involving all other proceedings constituted 8 percent of the total.

Table IV-3
Profile of Criminal Appeals Resolved by Opinion

Proceeding		Offense	
Jury Trials	44	Homicide	8
Nonjury Trials	20	Other Crimes v. the Person	36
Probation Revocation	5	Property	11
Guilty Pleas	23	Drug Sales or Possession	23
Other	8	Other	22
All Appeals	100%	All Appeals	100%

Appeal Processing—Briefs, Argument, Opinion Writing

Briefs

The number of briefs filed, the number of pages filed, and the number of issues raised are measures of appeal complexity. By these measures, the court's criminal caseload is overwhelmingly routine. Civil appeals, on the other hand, routinely have more than two briefs. Although criminal appeals are more likely than civil appeals to have only one issue, a much greater percentage of criminal appeals raise three or more issues. As briefs were unavailable, there are no data on median length of briefs.

Table IV-4
Briefing in the Appellate Division

	Civil	Criminal
Percentage of Cases with 2 Briefs Only	75	96
Percentage of Cases with 3 Briefs or More	25	4
Percentage of Cases with 1 Issue	68	56
Percentage of Cases with 2 Issues	24	18
Percentage of Cases with 3 or More Issues	8	27

Oral Argument

Whether an appeal is argued orally can also be a measure of case complexity. Oral argument, held in 50 percent of the appeals, is as frequent in criminal appeals as in civil appeals, largely as a result of the argument-without-briefs presentation on the sentencing calendar. In the remaining criminal appeals, the argument rate is 25 percent.

Opinion Writing

The court's writing practices are related to both judicial effort and time from submission to decision. As shown in Table 5, the court writes medium-length opinions, with published opinions being longer than unpublished opinions. Only a small fraction of its opinions are published, and separate concurrences or dissents are quite uncommon.

Table IV-5
Opinion-writing Practices

	Civil	Criminal	Combined
Median Length of Published Opinions (Pages)	9	7	9
Median Length of Unpublished Opinions (Pages)	4	4	4
Percentage of Published Opinions	8	3	5
Percentage of Dispositions with Separate Opinions	1		1

Appeal Times

The median time from notice of appeal to disposition in all appeals was 278 days. Civil appeals were resolved somewhat more quickly, 251 days as opposed to 329 days for criminal appeals. The faster times for all civil appeals represent more than a greater attrition. When appeals closed by decision are examined separately, the median time for civil appeals is markedly shorter than for criminal appeals: 308 days to 411 days.

Table IV-6
Median Disposition Times (Days)

	Civil	Criminal	Combined
All Appeals	251	329	278
Appeals Closed by Decision	308	411	318

The comparison of median times for each stage is shown in Table IV-7.

Several observations can be drawn from the times in Table IV-7. First, the largest part of total appeal time is consumed in preparing the transcript and the parties' briefs. Civil appeals are substantially faster in this preparation period, largely as a result of the longer time required by the public defender in ordering and obtaining the transcript and writing a brief. Second, a relatively small portion of total appeal time is consumed after the court has received those materials, and there are only modest differences between civil and criminal appeals. Third, decisions are handed down promptly after submission.

Table IV-7
Median Appeals Times by Stage of the Appeal

	Civil	Criminal
Notice of Appeal to Record	52	61
Record to Appellant's Brief	56	125 *
Appellant's Brief to Appellee's Brief	37	40 *
Appellee's Brief to Argument/Submission	95	98 *
Argument/Submission to Decision	23	11
Notice of Appeal to Decision	308	411

* Does not include appeals on the sentencing calendar. All appeals are included in the overall time on appeal.

Understanding Appeal Times

The court uses a variety of differentiated procedures to enhance judicial productivity and affect appeal time. The primary example is the sentencing calendar. While accelerating the court's consideration of a discrete category of appeals by scheduling on separate calendars and deciding these appeals by order, this procedure relieves resource problems of the public defender's office, which inhibit faster processing for criminal appeals. Times for criminal appeals would be considerably slower were it not for the sentencing calendar, used in one-third of the criminal appeals, which obviates the need for written briefs.

The court's extensive use of two-judge panels influences total appeal time for both civil and criminal appeals. The smaller panels enable the court to reduce the time from the close of briefing to argument or submission without argument, increasing the number of appeals heard each month without increasing the number of appeals on which each judge must sit.

Times between submission and decision may be affected by the form of the decision and opinion release practices. The shorter time from submission to decision for criminal appeals reflects the large volume of criminal appeals handled on the sentencing calendar, where appeals are resolved by order. For civil appeals, the difference in decision time for opinions ultimately published (a median of 50 as compared to 23 days) shows the effect of the judges' efforts without the time required for review (because the publication decision is not made by the court).

The scope and extent of the procedural and management innovations the court has adopted appear to be, in large measure, the result of its management structure, consisting of a long-tenured administrative presiding judge and this staff's support. This is a large court (the largest IAC of statewide jurisdiction) requiring active management.